SACRED REDESIGN

HOW TO FREE YOURSELF FROM SOCIETY'S STANDARDS AND CREATE HEAVEN ON EARTH

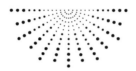

PUBLISHING

CONTENTS

INTRODUCTION

When the words *Sacred Redesign* came to me in the early morning, I knew it was the title for our next Amazon bestseller.

Either people have completely overhauled their life, business, family, and lifestyle over the last two years—or they have supported those who have.

What every single person will tell you is that they never imagined it would look like this, and it's so much better than they could have dreamed.

Now, there is always that messy middle that none of us enjoy, but it's part of the process.

Last winter, we were remodeling my grandparent's home, and it was common to have six or seven pickups in our driveway. The house was loud, dusty—and often felt chaotic.

One day, when harvest-gold shag carpet was being pulled out to make room for new wood floors, an absent-minded plumber carrying a new shower upstairs slammed into my grandma's beautiful ceiling tiles.

I had enough!

I stormed around the house and yard until I found Derek and I said, "That man is never allowed on this property again! EVER!"

He knew I was serious, and he was gone. Another contractor finished the upstairs bathroom and did a great job.

When I think back about what broke that day, it was the messy middle. Nothing was quite done. It was all mid-project.

There were times I was missing the leaking toilet and god-awful carpet because I couldn't see how great the new was going to be.

If you have ever been in the middle of a construction site that is called your life, you know it's daunting.

The courage, patience, and trust it takes to let one career go and create another...

To move from the city to the country...

To take your kids out of school...

To redefine what matters midlife...

It's not as simple or romantic as it sounds.

The contributors in this book have faced their fears, their demons, the critics, and sat in the dark with all the what ifs.

If you have braved this journey—or are in the middle of it—you will find comfort and inspiration in the pages of this book.

As I write this sitting at my farm table, with beautiful wood floors beneath my feet, new furniture in the living room, towers of veggies and herbs thriving, with a view of my favorite mountain, I can tell you the messy middle doesn't last forever.

You will find yourself looking back and then sinking into this moment feeling deep gratitude for the new reality you have created.

It feels heavenly, and you allow yourself to breathe it in.

No matter what's going on in the world, your life is yours to design. You can create heaven on earth with each thought, choice, and action.

This is the first book we have also included Body of 9 wisdom. This is a body-based way to know yourself. It is a very simple way to understand ourselves and how we relate to each other and the world. Martin and Susan Fisher have identified over 7,500 people—including each contributor in this book.

We are happy to say that all nine numbers are represented, and each shares their story and wisdom in their own unique way.

In the foreword, you will learn a little about each number, their values, and gifts. I can tell you how much opened up for me once I learned my number and what is true for me. It has also assisted me in my marriage and in parenting my children.

Each of us holds a beautiful piece of the puzzle. May this book remind you of this.

Blessings on the path,
Cheers to your sacred redesign!
Adriana Monique Alvarez

FOREWORD

The Body of 9 offers a context, a comprehensive, body-based process to better understand ourselves. We're continually informed by our physical bodies through nine distinct regions in the body that directly impact the way we experience our lives. We're each born with one of nine regions activated at birth. This active region is what we at Body of 9 call your Natural Number

Based on that active region, the body develops and presents distinct physical and spiritual characteristics, specifically in posture, movement, and structure, using specific muscles, bones, and fascia, and in energetic signature and purpose as well. These innate characteristics, which are governed by nature rather than nurture, directly determine how we relate to ourselves and others.

This is the first book of its kind—where all of the author's Natural Numbers have been identified and their wisdom presented in the context of their body and the corresponding purpose, skills, and gifts.

In context, the wisdom of each Natural Number is easier to understand and receive. Together as a whole, they make more sense, each Natural Number contributing a pearl of important wisdom. Each Natural Number, when active, offers something entirely different from the others. Here are the core benefits of learning each of the Natural Numbers:

1. Natural Number 1 honors others and treats them with respect, holding all equally, and providing each person with a sense of value.
2. Natural Number 2 engages with another person as they exist in the moment, without agenda.
3. Natural Number 3 experiences the intense joy and energy of togetherness at the pure soul-level of connection.
4. Natural Number 4 offers insight into self, in order to align with your core being and with others for a more intimate, authentic connection.
5. Natural Number 5 helps others to achieve their purpose, calms the mind, and reveals congruity between information and its source, whether to confirm or challenge its validity.
6. Natural Number 6 senses when and how to generate energy to move a group, project, or person into action, knowing what must follow to align with the greatest good for all involved.
7. Natural Number 7 effectively instigates change, opens minds to new possibilities, and optimizes the efficiency of these new potentials and processes.
8. Natural Number 8 uses the body to develop trust and shape integrity in ways that create safety for all. It grounds the creative process in realistic tasks and actions for different members of a group.
9. Natural Number 9 helps you know your place in the Universal flow, so that you can create efficiently with harmony and balance, without using excess energy or force to bring coherence.

NATURAL NUMBER 1

Natural Number 1 is about experiencing Source, where Source refers to the power of creation, the Cosmic Energy that creates life. They help us to feel, see, and share the awe, beauty and majesty of the world and the people within it. Deeply honoring and respecting others derives from this experience of Source.

Andrea Blindt shows us how vulnerability creates strength and resilience. She shows us that by drawing on the power that comes from the source of creation we can rebuild and redesign ourselves, even in the face of adversity and despair. There are times when we get caught in a place so dark, we think we can never escape, that there will be no end to the pain and suffering. Andrea found, through the connection available to the power of creation in her Natural Number 1 body that she could use this source to regenerate and start anew.

Camilla Fellas Arnold knows that creativity drives and heals us. When off her creative path, Camilla is disconnected from her purpose. As a Natural Number 1, she understands that words matter and that she has a gift and purpose related to communicating creatively. She is a champion of the creative process and its power to heal and grow.

Dina Marais inherently knows that all beings should be honored and treated fairly. Out of experiencing the opposite as a young person, she fell prey to what many Natural Number 1s do: self-doubt and unworthiness and attempting to control the uncontrollable. By opening to her connection to Source, learning to trust the perfection within her, and that this comes from Source, Dina found a way to honor herself and connect into the infinite power of that Source.

NATURAL NUMBER 2

Natural Number 2 is about connection through relationships to the magic in others. It is a merging with others, attuning with our whole being to the body of another person for the sake of connection alone. Natural Number 2 teaches us that everything starts with connection through active engagement and movement.

Derek Alvarez shows how when we fully engage in our life, anything can be created. As a Natural Number 2, It is through his relationships that he learns and expands his experiences. In his partnership with Adriana, Derek embraces the magic in the relationship, fully willing to jump into full engagement. It is this complete openness to new experience and appreciation of the people in his life providing those experiences that enables him to redesign his life over and over. By trusting the relationships with his loved ones and ultimately with himself, valuing the connections, and going all-in without fear, Derek has shown us how a fully engaged life can morph and change. As a Natural Number 2 he knows in his body that movement and engagement create a joyful life, and we don't need much more than having our basic needs met to have that for ourselves. We just need to show up and be ready for what is to come.

Melissa Chernow is one of the embodied Natural Numbers. Through connection and engagement with others, Melissa found her connection back to herself. She learned to trust her body's wisdom and to advocate for what she felt was true for herself and her body. By asking for real and true connection, honesty about our feelings, she found her way to expressing and listening to herself.

Michall Medina values connection. She calls us forward to show up as ourselves, be who we are unapologetically. As a Natural Number 2, she knows herself through her relationships, and it is through her gaining clarity about her relationship with herself that she finds her way through anxiety and isolation to connection and fulfillment.

Shunanda Scott starts her chapter with the acknowledgement that even when we are alone physically, we are never alone physio-spiritually. Whether with ourselves—with the Angels or with each other—if we open ourselves to engagement, magic happens. It is only when we actively restrict ourselves off from connection and the possibilities that are presented to us that we truly miss-out. Through connecting with others, Angels, and ourselves we can find and care for who we are.

NATURAL NUMBER 3

Natural Number 3 is about a focused connection to others that ignores the persona and goes straight to our being, our greater purpose, and using the joy of connection from that relationship to inspire us into action toward that purpose. They are the heralds of our being, announcing our purpose to the universe so that we may be included in the universal plan of manifestation and creation.

Shayna Melissa has tremendous focus. When a Natural Number 3 makes you the object of their focus, they are able to ask many detailed questions in order to build the larger picture. Shayna uses her Natural Number 3 ability to help others see new possibilities by researching and understanding the underlying details of her patient's physical health. She has consistently used her focus to learn and develop herself and her understanding of how to heal others naturally. She brings her tremendous ability to inspire and instill joy to move herself and her clients forward to a vision of health and enjoyment of life.

Terrie Silverman takes you on her journey. By sharing small details of her life, she builds a larger picture of her path to connecting into her purpose. As a Natural Number 3, she has the ability to inspire and move our soul into action. When she found her path, helping people tell the stories that light up their lives, bring forward their passionate purpose, and cheerlead them forward, it feeds her soul's purpose too! Terrie listens, recognizes, and champions others. As a Natural Number 3, she inherently knows that each person needs to be announced to the universe. She is a herald of our purpose and presence—announcing our being so that our lights shine within us and within the universe.

Tiffanie Yael Maoz reminds us that aligning our life and work with our soul's purpose is ultimately the most fulfilling path. Natural Number 3s inspire us to live toward the fullest future in front of us. Tiffanie continually points to how we can "transform to what really feels right at a soul level." This is the super-power of Natural Number 3—they can see what is possible for us, help us to envision and articulate that possibility and they energize us on the path toward to vision.

NATURAL NUMBER 4

Natural Number 4 is about our relationship to our infinite self, to our life-force within our being. Through knowing and accepting our timeless selves, we are ready to transform using our connection to our deepest life force energy. From there we find a place of alignment and authenticity.

Brad Walsh talks about how the powerful relationships in his life, with women in particular, have framed and developed his sense of himself. Throughout his growth and development, he uses his awareness of how he was feeling and how those feelings caused him to make a change. Natural Number 4s know who to connect with whom and how to build a network of connections that serve the greater good. That is where he is now, creating and strengthening his network of powerful women.

Camberly Gilmartin connected into the infinite source of wisdom within her early in her life. Natural Number 4s can connect into the limitless energy of life, lived or not. Camberly actively uses her Natural Number 4 ability to know who needs to be connected to whom for the purpose of creating together. She understands the importance of both physical and spiritual nutrition, nurturing so that growth can happen. She knows that we all have the seed of life within us.

Esther Lemmens knows we are all connected at the life force level. With that comes a built in knowing of when and to whom we are intimately connected, either in this lifetime or the last. In her nature she knows that she can also offer a deep sense of acceptance for who we are in the moment, and a deep intimacy of connection that starts easily. Esther demonstrates the knowing that we have an inner world inside us, and from here we can offer ourselves deeply and authentically. Natural Number 4s stay in the connection until it completes and has done what it was supposed to do. Esther models this way of being in her chapter. Esther also shows us that by finding the wisdom in our emotions we can escape the bonds that come from our nurture, our experiences, and our society, to find self-love and acceptance.

Georgina El Morshdy talks about the importance on knowing oneself. Her Natural Number 4 wisdom helps her know that we all have a deep inner wisdom inside of us. By trusting this connection to who we are at our deepest place, we can reestablish a healthy relationship with ourselves and the world around us, embrace our uniqueness, and live authentically.

NATURAL NUMBER 5

Natural Number 5 sets and holds the context for transformation—what do we know, what do we need to find out, how is what we know related to everything else and what are the relationships between people, knowledge and intuition that need to be taken understood? Natural Number 5s know that everything is interconnected, knowable and needs to be congruent to be accepted into the existing framework of understanding.

Brigid Holder demonstrates how Natural Number 5s hold a container for us to become what they can see is possible. Her chapter is all about her journey of doing that for herself, finding and living into one's greater purpose. Brigid follows her Natural Number 5 purpose to help us know there is more, that we have a greater spiritual purpose, and when we move relentlessly toward our bigger purpose, we can have our best life.

Dr. Kristina Tickler Welsome as a Natural Number 5 knows that we all have a spiritual nature. She reminds us that each of us is here to develop, protect and honor our own spiritual nature. She holds the container for all of us to find a way to explore and understand who we are, to take responsibility to connect to that part of us where the "more" in life can be found. Natural Number 5s know that it is our "birthright" to live with a conscious connection to who are at a spiritual level, reconnecting body mind and spirit to find our whole selves.

Martin Fisher, using his Natural Number 5 abilities, has been the holder and builder of the understanding of Body of 9. He is responsible for the context, consistency and congruency of the understanding around the nine Natural Numbers. He is a custodian of the knowledge, continues to build and expand the framework of understanding that is Body of 9.

Silke Harvey knows at the level of her Natural Number 5 being that we all have a spiritual nature. She can feel into and know what those around her need to hear, and hold a space for all to grow into the largest spiritual self. If we lose our connection to the lightness of our spiritual nature, Silke can help us re-capture it.

NATURAL NUMBER 6

Natural Number 6 points us in the most alive direction, providing the energy necessary for movement to overcome any inherent inertia. Natural Number 6s experience the energy present in a situation, they decode and magnify it back, so that everyone can tap into the energy of the moment.

Jolynn (Raven) Van Asten describes the details and aliveness of the world with the goal of helping you feel into the truth of the moment and to find a way to use this to energize yourself forward. She describes how the world constantly is knocking us off our center, making us doubt who we are and the value we offer. She helps us feel the sense of loss that we all face day-to-day, and then shows us that there is always another path, another way through to the aliveness of life, and it will show up in the present moment as what is most alive.

Susan Fisher as a Natural Number 6 feels, and synthesizes energy in the moment – this enables her to know the most alive direction, the next most important actions for a community or a person to take. Susan has developed her body's ability to discern a person's Natural Number – through both observation of attributes and by using her ability to feel what is happening in that person's body. She uses these keen observational skills combined with her ability to move humanity forward to be an energetic catalyst for change and growth.

NATURAL NUMBER 7

Natural Number 7 is about change, purpose, and possibility. People of this Natural Number see the unique purpose of a person, group, or community, and they can present possibilities that have not yet been envisioned that will move those involved toward their greatest purpose. They also enable us to leave behind that which no longer serves us to ensure that we can move forward toward our great vision and stay open to what we do not yet know. Change is inherent in transformation; Natural Number 7 helps us let go of what no longer serves, thereby creating space to open to new possibility.

Adriana Monique Alvarez, is as alluring as she is elusive, so full of potential, so protective of possibility. If you look in the dictionary for the definition of Natural Number 7, you should find a photo of Adriana. From the moment she was born—from the start of her story— Adriana lives the values of Natural Number 7 so clearly and consistently. Even through her transformation, she knows that she holds true to herself. Where the container has changed, the contents are still and always a bubbling mess of love, potential, and possibility and truth. How can we become that potential that Adriana holds out for us all to see if we hold on too tightly to our past? How can we grow into our next transformation if we are not brave, curious and boundary-less. This is what Adriana gifts to all of us—boundless freedom, fun, joy—*if* we are brave enough to embrace our fullness.

Anne Teijula weaves a common tale for our Natural Number 7s. They long for adventure and freedom. They will risk relationship to follow their adventurous spirit. In the care of loyal and true friends they can create a nest and blossom, inviting and embracing change at the turn of every season. From here they show us that anything is possible if we dare to follow our dreams, visions and stay open to possibility.

NATURAL NUMBER 8

Natural Number 8 guides us to move forward together to create with consideration and integrity for the benefit of all. Aligning the body with the physical source of creation, the earth, they draw energy into their body. Their body guides them to create an atmosphere ripe for growth.

Charli Fels starts her chapter with a picture of power, landing in our body what it feels like to be a modern powerful woman. She goes on to describe what it feels like to be constricted in the body by the world around us. She stands up against the idea that we must embrace our masculine in order to be powerful. She has a list of things that came from perseverance in the face of negativity. As a Natural Number 8, she holds strong for each of us to create ourselves and have the courage to persevere and to find the power within us.

Emmi Mutale is far more aware of the details of the ebb and flow of her body than people of the other Natural Numbers. She talks about her struggle with adrenaline addiction that Natural Number 8s often suffer from. They are stronger and have more endurance than the other Natural Numbers, and they will take themselves past the point of exhaustion into adrenaline override—for Natural Number 8s this is a version of creating a natural high. Safety is a core need and value for Natural Number 8s and when missing in youth can ripple through their life, often in the form of abdicating their natural power and losing connection and trust with their body. Emmi talks about how she got her body connection back.

Jennifer Spor's story is one of resilience. Jennifer uses her Natural Number 8 power and ability to get things done to get through tough circumstances over and over again. She overcomes abuse, addiction, and despair by continually finding the strength within her. She is straight forward, learns to hold boundaries, despite the challenges of not being able to protect herself as a child, she comes through by drawing on her natural abilities to succeed in the world, by the external definition. Then through those life lessons finds her unique power and ability within herself to follow her own path.

NATURAL NUMBER 9

Natural Number 9 holds the container for everything that exists. They are able to bring the transformation and change processes to completion and to release the energy to create again. Natural Number 9 understands how to include everything, create unity, and shepherd our human experience through the transformation process. They live within all that is, this makes their experience completely expansive. None of the other Natural Numbers contain everything; this makes it hard for others to comprehend the breadth and perceive the impact of Natural Number 9.

Asha Suppiah talks about the frustrations that Natural Number 9s feel when society wants to structure their infinite existence in a particular container. They know we are far more than our labels; in fact, the labels are more like points in space for Natural Number 9 rather than concepts that define us. Natural Number 9s often feel like they don't fit in with how society defines our behavior, and this is because they know they fit in the infinite, not necessarily the specific. They have big dreams and goals, and others cannot yet know the importance of what they see. Asha's journey is about expanding out and beyond the bounds placed on her into her true Natural Number 9-ness, and place of freedom and power.

Emily Tuck's superpower, that comes with Natural Number 9, is to know that we are part of all that is or ever was—on a visceral level. "We are everything," is a sentence that Natural Number 9 lives within. Emily, using the power of her Natural Number 9-ness and the knowledge of epigenetics, rearranges her DNA to transform her experience of life demonstrating the incredible power of Natural Number 9 to rearrange existence at a universal and cosmic level.

Sabrina Runbeck, as a Natural Number 9, understands that we are all inter-connected, that everything we do affects others. She knows the most efficient way to create change, and how to manifest in the universal field. She translates this understanding into practical advice to short-cut what might seem like a hard and challenging process to others, giving tips of how to network with more leverage. Natural number 9s teach that each of us is the fulcrum or balance point for our own lives—when we understand that we are our own center, we can choose the actions to create the greatest impact with the least effort. Sabrina's networking tips are just that, an option for creating great impact using networking as the tool.

ADRIANA MONIQUE ALVAREZ

The beginning of the end was the day the boys and I walked three blocks to Whole Foods like we did every single morning at 8 a.m.

This day was different. The streets were quiet. We walked through the sliding glass doors, and it felt like someone punched me in the gut. The produce section that was typically overflowing had been ransacked. There was not a single fruit or vegetable in sight. The boys stopped talking and being silly.

"What's wrong Mama?"

We walked each aisle and only found aluminum foil.

We took Magazine Street on our way home and every upscale boutique and shop had been boarded up.

I knew it was over.

We had been in New Orleans for eight glorious months. We found a gorgeous place in Uptown. We walked to Audubon Park on the daily. We had the famous St. Charles Ave just down the road. We had eaten like kings, and I even got to ride in Mardi Gras. The vibrant city whose music moved you like nothing else can, was dead.

We woke up to red chalk marks in front of our neighbor's house and learned this meant they were the next target to get robbed.

We were sitting ducks and we knew it.

We booked a flight to Mexico and prayed it wouldn't get cancelled. It did. We rebooked it and that one stuck.

The morning we left the special city of Nola we waited forty minutes for the one Uber driver who was working to pick us up. Everyone was terrified of the virus. We got to the airport, and we were the only people checking in.

A giant 747 flew us over the turquoise water, us and two other people. When we landed in Cancun, we had the beach to ourselves. I knew that had never happened in the history of Spring Break.

A few days later we drove to Merida and the lock downs were announced. No walking, no shopping, except for food, no music, no living. The city was silent, and we had nothing but time. Our beautiful AirBNB had a back yard that would become our medicine. The swimming pool, the patio furniture, and the huge lantana with bright pink flowers were what comforted me and kept me sane.

Over the next three months I became aware of what travel meant to me. As a little girl in my grandma's living room, I flipped through the pages of National Geographic, and I promised myself I would go. Pictures were not enough for me. I wanted to smell it and taste it. I wanted to walk down the streets and I wanted stories about my wild adventures.

As a nineteen-year-old I remember packing my bags and holding my ticket to Burma, feeling the absolute thrill of the unknown and the huge concern that I had no idea what I was doing.

At twenty-one I moved to Albania and that is where I became myself. Thousands of miles from home, I discovered who I was outside of anyone's definitions and demands. If it wasn't for travel, I would have never become me. I would have never remembered how capable and resourceful I am. I would have never known that I am quite good at communicating without knowing a single word of the language. I am a great packer, and I can sleep standing up on a train. I would have never lived on $300 a month or learned how good the chocolate in Belgium is. I would have never discovered life outside of my country. I wouldn't have learned that there was more to life than working and making money. And I would have never seen the most breathtaking sunsets on the Adriatic, walked through Italy's palaces, swam in the Greek Islands, or tasted perfectly ripe figs right off the tree.

Travel was my teacher, my muse, my therapy, my freedom, my everything. When people told me, oh just be grateful you traveled when you did, I wanted to slug them. It's easy to discount something that doesn't mean anything to us, but we never know what it means to another. After losing my daughter Nina, travel became my favorite way to navigate grief. Plus, she was born and buried in Albania so it became hard for me to consider that I might not get to visit my favorite country for the foreseeable future.

For three months in that Mexican pool, I grieved Nina again. I grieved the loss of travel. The loss of choice. My parents kept calling asking us to come home. I didn't want to. It felt like defeat. Like leaving home and finding my path took every ounce of courage I had. Going back felt like I failed. It felt like I was giving up on my dreams and myself. What pushed me to say yes was my boys. I didn't want them cooped up in a house for a year. That wasn't what they were used to, and it wasn't how it was going to be. If we moved to Colorado they could play outside every day. They could have friends and freedom.

I called my dad and said, we'll come. We started looking at properties to move to and then he suggested we stay at my grandma's house until we figured it out. That felt good and yet I would have never thought of it.

We took an epic road trip up the entire length of Mexico and when we pulled into grandma's driveway at 10 pm on that last day, I heard, you are home. I felt a mix of relief and sadness.

Just like I did after losing Nina, I tried my best to be present and appreciate what we had and yet I often found myself daydreaming about how life used to be before. I feel so much shame to say it, but I had a hard time seeing what and who I had, I could only see who and what was missing.

My husband Derek and sons Sam and Grant are truly the greatest gifts life has given me. In a world of Insta photo shopped models and fake happy lives, it's easy to forget that some people really do have something special.

Derek, oh Derek he's that for me. I have no idea what I did right to get him, but he's my best friend and the person who accepts me exactly as I am. He loved me when I was young and naive, he loved me when I was a new mother tired out of my mind, he loved me when I was grieving, and he loves this new version of me.

There's a James Morrison song, *I Won't Let You Go*, that describes Derek's kind of love. It's not convenient, it's solid. The chorus says:

If there's love, just feel it.
And if there's life, we'll see it.
This is no time to be alone, yeah
I won't let you go.

If the sky is falling.
Just take my hand and hold it.
You don't have to be alone,
Yeah, I won't let you go.

And if you feel the fading of the light.
And you're too weak to carry on the fight.
All your friends that you count on have disappeared.
I'll be here, not gone, forever, holding on.
I won't let you go.

This man won't let me go. It's because of his steadfast, insanely unconditional love that I have been able to even entertain the idea of redesigning my life and my dream.

My boys are the funniest, silliest, wildest boys ever. They are confident and constantly bringing me back to this moment. They have no filter and say the things I am thinking but have learned aren't appropriate. They are free and so themselves. They love me and they bring me so much joy. They love my stories and Angel spray at night. They enjoy oracle cards and crystals. They appreciate my food and often say my secret ingredient is love.

The first summer in Colorado I struggled. It was a mixed bag. I was wrestling with the idea of who I thought I would be at 40 and where I was. I was falling in love with my new life, but I wasn't sure I liked the idea of it costing me my old life.

The first winter I decided I was done with grief clouding my joy and I chose to be present for longer. Less breaks from the happy moments with these three. I held their eye contact. I stayed in the activity. I didn't leave for some silly reason to wonder if I deserved them or this beautiful life.

The next summer I was all in. Jeep rides, swimming in the lake, kayaking, picking wild raspberries, picnics, sunrises and sunsets. I didn't give suffering any airtime. I found the more I was in nature, the more capacity I had for joy. The more I began to believe that my new life was pretty damn good. The party continued into fall and winter.

As the tulips and daffodils are popping up around the yard, I feel nothing but joy for this new life we have designed. There's a contentment that I remember from times gone by.

Right before I moved to Albania, I attended a survival course in the middle of the Florida swamps. There was basic housing, no electricity or plumbing. I spent my days taking care of goats and a pig. We cooked everything from scratch and went to bed with the sun. After thirty days, I was the calmest and grounded I had ever been. I didn't want it to end. I slept so well and felt connected to everything in this expansive Universe.

I moved just a few weeks later to Tirana and moved into a state-run orphanage that wasn't much different than that Florida training ground. When I talk about those early days in Albania, I have nothing but love for them. We had electricity and running water for only a few hours a day. We had limited food at the market, but those were the good ol' days! Life was simple and so good.

Interestingly enough, I never thought life in the U.S. could ever be this rich and peaceful, but it is now. We live six hours from any civilization. The property is tranquil. The breeze blows through the fruit trees Derek has planted. The dogs and cats run the yard. The boys are happy. Food is slow and from scratch. We are connected to the season, the temperature, the rain. We go to bed with the sun, and we rise with it. We grow our own herbs and veggies. Our neighbor raises our cow. There is no traffic or noise. We have everything that matters.

I don't need to go anywhere although I love my grandparents cabin an hour down the gravel road. I don't need an adventure, I'm living my best one. I am as free as I've ever been. I can finally see who and what's here instead of what and who isn't. I can finally see I didn't fail. I didn't miss my boat. I was always on it.

That little girl on grandma's floor could never have imagined she would take over. That she would become the mother who cooks for everyone and hosts the holidays. She would have never dared to ask for a life this good. She just kept putting one foot in front of the other. She kept choosing her heart over logic. She kept dreaming big, she kept scaring the shit out of everyone with her daring, dreaming ways. She kept trusting life. She kept accepting the love of those around her. She kept believing in the next and the next. Stitch by stitch her life became a masterpiece of her own design and its heaven on earth.

ABOUT THE AUTHOR

Imagine a world without gatekeepers and censorship. *This* is what inspired Adriana Monique Alvarez to start AMA Publishing, and train a global network of female-owned publishing houses. She's a USA Today bestselling author, and can be seen in *Forbes, Entrepreneur, Huffington Post, International Living, America Daily Post, London Daily Post,* and *Grit Daily*.

She is currently living in "the middle-of-nowhere" Colorado, where she is renovating her grandparents' home, and learning how to homestead with her husband, Derek, and two sons, Sam and Grant.

Website: *www.AdrianaMoniqueAlvarez.com*

2

SUSAN AND MARTIN FISHER

This is the story of an American woman and an Englishman, born thousands of miles apart, who grew up less than a hundred miles apart, one in Brussels, Belgium, and the other in Southend-On-Sea, England. Through a series of serendipitous events, both migrated to California, where they met and became friends. Sometimes in life you know when someone is important to you—these two felt a sense of destiny, but the timing was not quite right. They lost touch for 13 years, each travelling a tough road that was to prepare them for what was to come. This is the story of their journey.

In setting some context for both this book and this chapter, we hope you will consider holding a beginner's mind. Our experience has shown that much more is possible for us all if we choose 'Not to Disbelieve.' Start by clearing your mind, suspend disbelief, and enjoy the journey.

THE AWAKENING OF CHILDHOOD - SUSAN

Susan Bennett Fisher (nee Susan Gail Van Horn) was born in Baltimore, Maryland. At the age of 10, her family moved to Belgium when her father was offered a position managing a technical organization for ITT. She attended St John's International school where she combined academic success with a passion for sports and a curiosity for life.

"During my time at St John's International School, I learned French and German, traveled extensively, and played sports against all of the international schools in the neighboring countries. Through this experience, I was exposed to international cultures, foods, and belief systems, which broadened my perspective. I travelled extensively with my family and school, visiting India, Kenya, Tanzania, Israel, almost all the countries in Europe, and parts of Russia. This ignited my interest in learning and exploring and opened my eyes to the vast cultural differences and opportunities available in the world. During this time, I had several experiences that, as I look back now, were part of a possibility for spiritual awakening and awareness, but that were never nurtured, acknowledged or supported.

When I was 12, I had my first cosmic experience. I had fought with my younger sister over who would sit where to watch our favourite television show. I got so mad that I punched her in the arm, pretty much as hard as I could. It was a bit foolish, as my mother was sitting there too, and she promptly sent me to my room. Still steaming mad, I opened my window and crawled out onto the ledge. It was a truly wondrous star-filled night. As I sat there, communing with the Universe, with all of the cosmos stretched out before me, a voice started to communicate with me. It told me that I was very powerful and had a great purpose, but that I would need to learn to direct the power of my energy for good; that I should never lose control and use that level of force against others as I came into my power.

I never told anyone about this experience; instead, I held it as a guide for my actions going forward. It was an intensely personal and powerful experience of the "more" that is out there. I stored it away, along with the knowing of how magical our existence could be.

I didn't choose to believe, and I didn't choose to disbelieve—I accepted the experience as a knowing that came with my version of existence. If I had known my Natural Number at the time, this experience would have made more sense, and I would probably have explored it more openly as time went on. But I didn't know. I had no context for this experience; it was not until many years later that I understood what I had done to create it.

There were other moments, in the great Cathedrals of Europe, when I would feel the wisdom in the energy contained within, it was obvious to me that my experience was different than that of my family. At 16, in the Holocaust Museum in Jerusalem, I got lost in the murmurings of the victims, while wandering through the piles of hair and shoes rescued from Germany. I tapped my power and strength and again understood that it must be used for the good of others—nothing like this should ever happen again. These were times when I again had the sensation that I was being prepared, that I had a greater purpose, and that I held everything I needed within me.

These were formative experiences where I felt a deep connection to the universe, and to my power and purpose."

THE AWAKENING OF CHILDHOOD - MARTIN

"I was born near London, England. At an early age, my family moved to Southend-On-Sea, a town famous for the world's longest public pier, stretching over a mile out over the mudflats into the Thames River. Although my childhood passions were all connected to airplanes and flying, I found I had an interest and talent for computer programming while at a local high school. My interest in flying was nurtured at airports, airshows and events around England and the continent—I had a knowing that flying could take me closer to my spiritual nature.

Sacred Universe interaction number 1:

When I was 12, I had my first spiritual interaction. Perhaps because I was attending Sunday school and was absorbing the lessons from both Testaments, I wasn't surprised when I heard (in my mind) a voice offering support and guidance, communication with this entity being assured with a simple (secret) physical motion. From that moment on, I have been mostly fear-free.

After graduating from high school, I enrolled at Manchester University, one of the few Computer Science degree courses that didn't require building your own computer, graduating with an Honors Degree after the traditional three years. Like Susan, our education at that time was designed to prepare us for life working for a company, and I followed suit, trying to find my way.

THE DESCENT INTO OBLIVION – SUSAN

After high-school graduation, Susan left Europe and enrolled at Brown University.

"In 1978, I returned to the United States to study Mathematical Economics and Computer Science at Brown University. I joke sometimes that this was the best mistake I ever made—it started me down a path with a specific definition of success that I had grown up with. It was based on an expectation that I would succeed in business. After graduating, I started a two-year career adventure in financial systems in New York City. I found both the career and life in New York to be empty and hard. When I was accepted into the inaugural class of the Lauder Institute, a combined MBA/MA offered by the Wharton School and University of Pennsylvania's School of Arts and Sciences, I jumped at the chance to reconnect with my international roots, hoping to find some greater significance there than I had found in my first foray into business.

The program was designed to develop business language proficiency and cultural sensitivity in its graduates, and to some extent, it did provide a greater sense of purpose. Wharton Business School in the 1980s was in full-form teaching how to make money using leverage, aka other people's money. It was a form of brainwashing, defining success as money and power, and I bought in. From there, I pursued a varied career in consulting, marketing, engineering management, and operations, working 60 hours or more a week. I thought I had "made it"; I got married, had three daughters, made money, did everything that had been prescribed by my education and expectations. And I completely lost touch with myself, that connection to a purpose, that sense of significance I had felt in my youth."

THE DESCENT INTO DISTRACTION – MARTIN

Sacred Universe interaction number 2:

"After University, I accepted a job as a programmer, not yet knowing that life was about to give me a serious nudge. One Sunday afternoon, I was reading the newspaper and randomly saw an advertisement with a picture of the Golden Gate Bridge and an offer of work in Silicon Valley if the candidate had experience or qualifications that matched a long list of software disciplines. It seemed that the advertisement was talking to me. The list matched my degree courses almost exactly, and I decided right then that I was going to America! Three months later, I landed in San Francisco with the two other successful candidates. I spent 4 years working at that company, until early one morning my manager came into my office and told me that they were looking for volunteers to be laid-off, but I'd need to let him know by lunchtime. I said yes before he reached the door. Within 4 days of leaving that company, I was hired by Oracle, employee number 330 or so.

After working for Larry Ellison at Oracle for almost 4 years I left to try my luck at a number of start-ups, all of which failed. I had started working as a consultant, hired by Tom Siebel, who went on to build Siebel Systems, and there I met Susan.

For a couple of years, Susan and I would have lunch and play bridge with a couple of her friends and chat in the hallways. We both felt a connection but didn't yet have the timing, skills, life experience, or means to build our relationship beyond that point. After she became pregnant with her second child, her job moved to Oakland, and my job had me travelling most of the time. We lost touch and didn't see each other for 13 years.

Meanwhile, in 1996 I received an unexpected call from a recruiter, offering me an interview with a new company called Yahoo!. I was hired on as employee number 100 and for 4 years lived an unreal lifestyle at the height of the dot-com boom. I got to knock big things off my bucket list. I bought a number of airplanes; I married my college crush at Pebble Beach; I flew myself and a close group of friends to Hawaii. The experience of having unlimited resources was exhilarating. But deep down, I somehow felt that I didn't deserve this bounty.

Then came the dot-com bust and everything evaporated in front of me. All that was easy became hard and empty. I was forced to file for bankruptcy and go back to living in a place where I depended on every paycheck. I had to rebuild from scratch.

But the lessons learned were priceless. I learned about the value of money, friends and family who stood by me, who remained true, and what was important.

THE RE-AWAKENING – SUSAN

"I first met Martin in Silicon Valley in 1991 where we were working together in a tech start-up. Despite the immediate connection we had and the friendship that we built, the initial timing for our connection wasn't right. We both had deep personal journeys to go on in the meantime, and we lost connection for 13 years. During this time, I continued a career in technology, focusing on the implementation of systems in operations and finance, and I also gave birth to and raised three daughters.

In my late-30s, with my three young daughters, I took stock of life. The path to success that had been laid out for me by my parents and educational institutions no longer held my truth. I wanted to be able to raise my children myself and not turn that task over to others or my increasingly sick husband. I also knew that there were many things fundamentally wrong with my marriage. Somehow my vision of our perfect family had disintegrated into pain and chaos, and I didn't know how or why that had happened. I knew that I was in very deep, way over my head, and I couldn't see a way out.

At this point, 9 years into an abusive marriage with a drug addict/alcoholic, I had lost any sense of myself. Every instinct, knowing, or intuition that might have guided me out of this deep hole had been groomed out of me. When I look back on this period, I can't imagine how I lived through it.

Al-Anon was the first step in my Sacred Redesign. Because of the embedded secrecy around abuse, I had been raised in a family system where alcoholism and abuse were the foundation of a relationship. It wasn't actively alive in my immediate family, but it was the underpinning of how I had been raised in multi-generational systems of abuse that were never spoken of. At this point, I had spent years under the thumb of a master groomer, who continually knocked me off my center, so much so that I had lost myself. Through Al-Anon, I took my first steps back to finding my personal power and left my husband.

I began to study to become a Life Coach with The Coaches Training Institute in San Rafael, California. I was encouraged by my coach to begin their Leadership Program. In this program, my Natural Number was identified. The experience broke open the floodgates that had been restricting me for most of my adult life. The rush of energy and power that I felt after having my Natural Number identified was physically palpable. I knew that I had found my calling in life and found a way to connect with and love myself again.

From 2003 until 2012, I studied everything I could about this experience. I worked with the couple who had originally noticed the nine physiologies, Alan Sheets and Barbara Tovey of New Equations. I took all of their courses, volunteered, and spent as much time in the community of people exploring this discovery as I possibly could. From within this study, I reconnected to who I am, found simple physical ways to empower myself, and learned so much about the other Natural Numbers. I got everyone in my family identified, and immersed myself in learning."

THE RE-AWAKENING – MARTIN

Sacred Universe interaction number 3:

"The experience of losing everything—my fortune, my wife, my career —set me on a search for greater meaning in my life. I explored a great variety of spiritual disciplines, connecting into a local Christian community. Once again, while I was sitting calmly considering my future, my guide reappeared and quite forcibly said, "this isn't the right path for you, be patient."

Sacred Universe interaction number 4:

Months later, I was in Southend for my parents' 50th wedding anniversary. After celebrating with them, I went to see a friend, and we sat catching up over a few beers. Suddenly I heard (again in my mind) my guide insist I send a text to another friend of mine, Rachel, in Santa Cruz, California, to say hello. So, I did. I wasn't expecting a quick response; I was 8 hours ahead and it was 6 p.m. in California, but she immediately replied that she wasn't ok; she needed major surgery, but she was glad to hear from me. I made sure I stopped to see her on my way back home and discovered her friends had created a group for her support, where we could share news and encourage Rachel and each other. One of the group members was… Susan. The group had lunch a few days before Rachel's surgery, and I met Susan for the first time in 13 years. It wasn't as profound as I think either of us hoped, but we were at least reconnected. Rachel had her surgery and made a complete recovery.

Sacred Universe interaction number 5:

One October day, I called Rachel and suggested we meet for a celebratory dinner. She immediately agreed and asked if it would be ok if she invited Susan. Remembering the previous lunch, I agreed but with no expectations. At dinner, Rachel arrived with Susan, who was spectacular —she blew me away. On my long drive home, that voice spoke again "She said she was ready for a new relationship THREE times." Immediately, I called Rachel, got Susan's number, and called her. Finally ready for the big commitment, we were married within months—this was our first very big step on our now combined journey of Sacred Redesign."

AN INTRODUCTION TO NATURAL NUMBERS

Once they were spending time together, Susan introduced Martin to the ideas that New Equations was pursuing, and Martin was the first person that Susan identified on her own. It was a sweet moment for both of them, which solidified their relationship and ignited Martin's curiosity. The idea that there are nine distinct physio-spiritual types of human earth-suits was a revelation, and fit into Martin's Natural Number 5 world framework.

To Martin the basic premise of nine different Natural Numbers, nine ways of being, nine different body-types had merit, but the explanations and conjectures presented seemed mostly incomplete, and it took a further few years before Martin was able to be confident that he understood and could describe and teach this new reality.

"The catalyst of this change from slightly understood theory to practical implementation started in 2012 when we went to the Burning Man Festival, a 65,000-person festival in the Black Rock desert. At this festival, we offered Natural Number Identification as a gift to anyone who came and asked to know. The gifting culture, combined with the sacred nature of the experience, inspired us to continue to offer the physical identification experience free of charge to anyone who asked. This was the second big step on our journey of Sacred Redesign that we took together. In a place where I could be anything, I learned that I wanted to be me. I found my role and purpose as a partner with Susan in what has become Body of 9."

After returning home from Burning Man the first year, we realized that a whole new way of being had opened for us. Part came from the Burning Man experience, but the truly transformative part was working with the most beautiful part of people, connecting with them in their power through their nature, through the Natural Number Identification process.

We started taking our Body of 9 Camp (then known as 9 Energies) to festivals all over California. We attended Burning Man five times, Lucidity Festival four times, and a myriad of other festivals. From 2012-2015 we worked with as many people as possible. The repetition, the mistakes we made, the process of correction, and the personal growth that we both were experiencing kept inviting us to focus our full attention on this work.

From this research, Natural Number has been shown to be evident in people of 42 nationalities, all races, and all ages from babies to senior citizens.

From study, conversation, and anecdote with these thousands of individuals, we have distilled the core commonalities that apply to each of the Natural Numbers—their focuses, their gifts, and their challenges—in terms that resonate powerfully for each group. Our descriptions reflect the language, energy, and core values as described by a Natural Number's own members. The words are chosen carefully, as is how the information is presented. As a result, in the cases where we have worked hand-to-hand with new participants, we have been able to describe their life experience with an accuracy that surprises them and their friends who are there to observe.

The phenomenon can also be observed in how people "lead" their movement from different regions of their body and in the different ways that bodies develop. For example, in the body of a person with Natural Number 3, you see a raised and rounded clavicle where the top rib goes underneath the clavicle and connects to the manubrium. While we are not sure if the act of lifting at the manubrium, the natural movement of a person with Natural Number 3, creates this raised collarbone, or the raised collarbone is there to support that lifting of the manubrium, but it is something that we consistently see in the body of Natural Number 3s.

When seen repeatedly among members of a group with the same Natural Number, the physiological differences become increasingly visible and pronounced. We were able to expand these points of reference particularly at festivals, where we would work with up to 100 people per day. The repetition of people with the same primary Natural Number showed us the specific patterns in each of the physiologies.

The data gathered to date supports our theories and assertions. For instance, observations show that no one in a nuclear family (parents and their biological children) shares the same Natural Number until there are more than nine people in a family. The eighth and ninth child share the Natural Number of their parents, and there is some evidence that children from the tenth on start to repeat the same sequence already represented in the family order.

The geographic distribution by Natural Number around the world appears generally uniform, although some events, gatherings, or professions seem to attract more of certain Natural Numbers than others.

We have learned that people of each Natural Number use the same words to express vastly different concepts and physical sensations. Often, it is only through activation of a Natural Number region in the body that a person can truly begin to comprehend the physio-spiritual experience that informs another's use of language to describe their perception. If ignored, this reality holds a possibility of miscommunication.

OUR EVOLUTIONARY ADVANTAGE

This experience, researching and learning to activate all nine regions of our body, interacting with people at their most authentic and deepest level has completely transformed our experience of ourselves, our relationships and our connection to the world, Universe, and Source. With this work, we continue to evolve, expand and improve our understanding of ourselves, our gifts and skills, and the ability to hear and receive the gifts of others. Our love story is still just beginning—and now we grow together in partnership toward a new possibility for ourselves and for humanity. We are grateful that we are together, and that we have been given the chance to research and now contribute to humankind's evolution. We strongly feel that we've been supported by 'the universe' along our journeys, both before we were finally together and of course since.

WHAT ARE THE BODY OF 9 AND THE NATURAL NUMBERS?

The Body of 9 offers a comprehensive, body-based system that enables us to better understand ourselves and others. We're continually informed by our physical bodies through the nine distinct regions in the body that directly impact the way we experience our lives. We're each born with one region that's activated at birth. This active region is what we call our Natural Number.

Early in 2022, we realized that getting your Natural Number identified and gaining awareness of how you activate and uses your Natural Number is actually the first step on an evolutionary path for humanity. Knowing your Natural Number allows the process of change, of Sacred Redesign to commence.

Each Natural Number region of the body is comprised of a set of muscles, bones, and fascia. When activated through posture, attention, and intention, a shift occurs in our processing that affects how the primary senses are decoded, and allows access to other physical and nonphysical information sources. This provides different information and perspective to a person, depending on which region is activated.

Each person also grows through different life experiences that shape their reality and determine the "nurture" influences of their life. However, how they process these experiences, and how they engage with the world is directly and intimately connected to their primary physiology described by their Natural Number.

YOUR NATURAL NUMBER IS THE MOST INFLUENTIAL FORCE IN SHAPING HOW YOUR BODY DEVELOPS, WHO YOU BECOME, AND HOW YOU EVOLVE

Your Natural Number determines how you move. We all initiate our movement from our Activation Region. When people move in harmony with their nature, it feels highly supportive of the body, and it can be very beautiful to witness.

Your Natural Number impacts how you interact with other people. For example, those with Natural Numbers 1, 2, 3, and 4 use their eyes as part of the relationship-connection creation process, to actively build a specific type of relationship related to their Natural Number. Those with Natural Numbers 5 through 9, conversely, do not use direct eye contact as part of the activation of their Natural Number. They use them to observe.

Your Natural Number impacts how you interact with Source or Spirit, or whatever you call that energy that surrounds us and is greater than us. Each Natural Number connects and interacts with a different aspect of Source energy in a completely different way. For example, Natural Number 7 connects to infinite wisdom. Natural Number 6 feels the Source energy present in everything that exists. How each Natural Number experiences the world is explained more in depth in our books.

Your Natural Number is reflected in your face and body. Each of the Natural Numbers has a particular expression that shows when active. The quality in the eyes and the facial muscular hold is impacted by the active Region, and indicates which Natural Number is present. Body structure also varies depending on your Natural Number. For example, people of Natural Number 6 have expanded and lifted rib cages and a relatively flat and firm sternum. People of Natural Number 9 have a wider and more open upper chest area and more developed musculature along the spine, most visible when the arms are set back in the Natural Number 9 Posture of Activation. These distinct physiological differences are part of what we use to discern a person's Natural Number.

Your Natural Number also affects how you take in and process information. If you are exploring the activation of the other energies, your senses function according to which Region is active. For example, the eyes of someone with Natural Number 3 have a much greater ability to focus and narrow in, so that they view their surroundings in a much more concentrated way. Those with Natural Number 5 have a 360-degree awareness, which allows them to hear and follow what is going on all around them. What we perceive in our environment is shaped by the region or Natural Number that is activated.

And here is the paradox: each person brings their unique wisdom into the world, and it is both focused on and sourced from the activation of their Natural Number in the body. This wisdom best achieves its universal relevance when understood in the context of all nine Natural Numbers.

Having your Natural Number identified is an affirming experience that contributes to a process of growth. If you liken it to cultivating a tree, the identification process is akin to planting the seed. The seed has been introduced to an environment that will allow it to begin sprouting roots, and transition into a new state of existence. A great deal of work and support lie ahead before it becomes a fully formed tree; the seed will require water, nutrients, sunlight, and safety to grow, but the journey has begun. The roots systems will become more robust and complex, and a sapling will soon break the surface to change the landscape above.

When you have your Natural Number identified, a seed of understanding is planted in your being that will continue to grow on its own, sparking your own Sacred Redesign. Knowing your Natural Number can instill or restore a sense of stability and logic to your life. We see people become more content and aligned with their values and sense of purpose following their first intentional activation.

Once you have a conscious awareness of your Natural Number, your relationship with yourself will begin to shift. The core aspects of your strengths and perceptions come forward; some describe this as "your soul taking the lead". We also describe it as activating your neutral Observer. This enables you to look at your beliefs and behaviors from a new vantage point in order to make more informed decisions regarding your identity. This is one of the primary benefits of knowing your Natural Number.

Another major benefit is expanding your capacity to perceive and learn. Your body-based ability to take in and absorb information will sharpen, as will your comprehension and synthesis of that information. New information, potential, connection, and transformation become possible.

The identification process is a unique experience for everyone. When the power within you is first awakened, so too is the feeling of assured-ness in this reality. It is a novel and validating physical awareness of your natural power and capabilities.

Just as a gardener must be attentive to their plants to nurture them into full bloom, so too can a person nurture the development of their conscious access to the skills, values, and strengths of their Natural Number.

The more you cultivate your connection to your Natural Number, the stronger and more accessible it will become. Doing so provides:

- a simple physical process that lets you connect back to your core being
- a body-based ability to recover when you are triggered with emotions that take you to an un-present state
- a new understanding of what it means for you to be present
- the ability to activate your conscious neutral Observer—to view your actions from a non-attached perspective

In addition, using the skills and strength of your Natural Number enables you:

- to see, understand, and consciously choose your behaviours

- to learn the pitfalls of attributing motive to the behaviours of others based solely on your perspective
- to understand that eight out of nine other people do not 1) experience life the way you do, 2) perceive what you perceive, 3) understand what is obvious to you, or 4) care about that which you consider essential, and to recognize that the reverse is also true

When understood, this can create a new level of compassion and possibility for communication. We can stop making up what we think other people mean, and use curiosity to begin to explore others' intent and thinking.

All of this translates to better, deeper relationships, matched with a more profound acceptance of yourself and how your body informs you of your life experiences. As your understanding of yourself and others undergoes this metamorphosis, you are empowered to approach the complexity of life with confidence in your value, and the value of those around you. It is the start of your own Sacred Redesign.

Once your primary Natural Number has been identified, introspection will follow, examining and comprehending the wholeness of your being. You can then learn how to use your body to activate your primary Natural Number consciously, using the muscles, bones, and fascia that already function as sensors for the bulk of your experience.

Each Natural Number offers a particular gift in the community. Your presence alone brings the impact and benefit of your Natural Number to each person in the community. The nine together, when consciously contributed, are designed to function as a working whole:

1. **Natural Number 1** brings in new energy from the Source of creation, aligning all present to their Source-level selves.
2. **Natural Number 2** creates the connection needed for each of us to hear, receive, and respond to one another.
3. **Natural Number 3** activates our soul, enabling us to give our gift from our highest purpose.
4. **Natural Number 4** connects us into the place where we are all

connected, the Source of life, so we remember that when we create, it must be done in alignment with who we are as a collective and as individuals.

5. **Natural Number 5** helps us know what is known and what we need to find out; to know where we are and what is possible from what we already know.
6. **Natural Number 6** energizes the transformation process and moves the community forward in the most alive direction.
7. **Natural Number** 7 ensures that we let go of what is not of service and remain open to new possibilities. They hold the larger vision for the community.
8. **Natural Number 8** enables us to use the power of our bodies and the earth to protect, nurture, and support the growth needed to bring the transformation to fruition.
9. **Natural Number 9** helps to bring the human process to conclusion, metabolize the experience, and free the energy of the transformation process to begin again in a way that includes everything.

Activating the Other 8 Natural Numbers

Knowing your own Natural Number is only the first step of the journey. If one considers that activating one's own Natural Number is like fine tuning to your radio station to remove the static, activating the other Natural Numbers (we each have all 9 in our body) is like adding 8 new stations one can tune in.

Activating all the Natural Numbers also lets you deeply experience your own magic and gifts, and helps you see how fundamentally different you are than the other 8 Natural Numbers.

Humans are physical creatures. We improve our bodies through physical action. For example, reading a book or even watching a video on how to play tennis won't teach you how to return a tennis ball across the net. You'll have a general sense, but will require physical practice to reliably play the game. Learning to activate all nine regions in your body is a similar physical practice, one that enables you to perceive, and to some extent share, the physical reality of others. It reaches towards that same goal of connecting with people of different minds, but through a body-based series of exercises that we can physically feel and comprehend.

While the discoveries of our research may seem to be unlikely, the experience and truth from the 8,000+ people that have contributed to our body of knowledge assures us of the accuracy of our new understanding of our human experience.

This book is the first of its kind. Each author has had their Natural Number Identified and their story is set in the context of their Natural Number at the outset of each chapter. Understanding where a person comes from in their perspective, the gifts they offer and the values they hold can help you see the world through their lens, and to hold what they offer as a gift to you, a shift to another perspective. You personally may not care about what is important to them, but by staying open and curious, you can expand your perspective to include theirs in a new way—each of us has something important and potent to offer. Use your beginner's mind and stay open to what is being offered—you may be surprised by the impact!

ABOUT THE AUTHOR

Susan Bennett Fisher and Martin R. Fisher are pioneers in the study and research of the 9 Natural Numbers. With over 30 years of combined research and experience with Body of 9, their work has led to many discoveries and a deeper understanding of the importance, power, and impact of knowing your Natural Number and learning to consciously use this aspect of your body. Since 2012, Susan and Martin Fisher have been working together to identify over 8,000 people from around the world and to build and share the understanding of how the Body of 9 shows up in so many aspects of human experience. Today they work with Coaches and Holistic Practitioners to bring in new information and new abilities to perceive so that coaches can create a new playing field for their clients. Body of 9 adds evolutionary skills, tools, and awareness that change coaches and their clients forever.

Like the Myers Briggs Personality Assessment, the Enneagram, or other personality identification systems, the Body of 9 enables you to better understand who you are and what your strengths and skills are. Body of 9 differs in that it is body-based—it is the shape, tone, and energy of your body that tells you which of the "types" you are. Body of 9 enables you to consciously develop and use the wisdom, strength, and power embedded in who you are, for *your evolutionary advantage*.

Website: *www.bodyof9.com*
Facebook: *www.facebook.com/Bodyof9*

3

ASHA SUPPIAH

Who are you?

I mean who are you really? Who are you beyond all the conditioning society has put on you?

That's the big question I have grappled with all my life. As a child of immigrant parents, I often questioned who I was. All I could see was society's labels: brown, Indian, second-generation Canadian, female, minority, person of colour. All I could see were who those labels required me to be: smart, obedient, disciplined, good at science, doctor/engineer/lawyer, perfect.

For me, these labels (and all they entailed) boxed me into an identity that didn't match me at all. I spent decades trying to reconcile the disconnect between who I was supposed to be and who I really was inside. From the confusion came a sense of self-doubt, frustration and unhappiness, which I just could not shake off for years.

Unfortunately, my story isn't an outlier or unusual in any way. For generations, women have been told to abandon themselves for the expectations of society. We are told who to be in every situation. We are told who we have to be in order to be a good daughter, a good mother, a good wife, a good daughter-in-law.

For centuries, women have been made to believe that who they are inside does not matter. Women have been taught that the only path to success is inauthenticity.

This is my cautionary tale of the cost of inauthenticity and how I found my way back through freeing myself from society's standards.

THE GOOD INDIAN GIRL

It was Grade 6, and my parents were at my school for the annual parent-teacher conference. Teachers hold this meeting to allow parents to come in to discuss their child's academics and functioning at school.

I still remember this day like it was yesterday. My parents and I walked into the classroom, and my teacher greeted us and asked us to sit down at the desk set up for the meeting. So began a fateful conversation:

Teacher: "Asha is doing incredibly well at language arts. She's at the top of the class."

My parents: "How about in science and math?"

Teacher: "Asha's doing pretty good but I would say her strongest subject is language arts. She's talented."

This one event changed the trajectory of my life forever. To my parents, the admission from my teacher was like *red lights* screaming "my daughter is not conforming with the archetype of a good Indian daughter." A good daughter of Indian immigrants gets perfect grades in science and math and becomes a doctor/engineer/lawyer.

I was immediately enrolled in the regional science fair, maybe with the hopes that this could improve my science grades. Fast forward 6 years and I had qualified to attend five national science fairs and won three gold medals, two silvers medals, and tens of thousands of dollars in special awards. Winning these awards made everyone around me believe I was really good at science and engineering. I was celebrated across Canada as one of the brightest scientific minds in the country—even receiving letters from the Prime Minister.

To the world, I looked like a genius kid, but inside I was incredibly insecure. I felt like a total fraud. Yes, it was true that I was "killing it" at science fairs, but my high school marks averaged in the 80s. I even had a few grades in the 70s *GASP*!

So, was I a "smart" kid? All my competitors at the national science fairs had high school averages in the high 90s. I absolutely loved most things about participating in the science fairs but did feel out of place when my competitors talked about their grades. I just sat there silently because they assumed my grades were as high as theirs since I was winning so many awards at the fair year after year.

Here's the truth: my parents were proud of my success at science fairs, but my grades in school always cast a cloud on my identity as a "good Indian girl."

I never quite felt good enough. I tried and tried and tried to fit into the identity of a "good Indian girl," but I just couldn't.

So, who was I really?

I was a passionate teenager who cared about making the world a better place. I was really good at developing creative ideas, testing them out, sharing my understanding with others and helping people see the value my ideas had for making a better world. I was so passionate about solving the world water crisis that I invented and patented a revolutionary technology to cheaply produce clean drinking water using two natural resources: the sun and seawater. I was not the kid with the best grades out there, but I was the one with the most passion and drive.

NOT YOUR TYPICAL STUDENT

"I'll be away at the national science fair next week so I will be missing the test. Can I schedule a date to do the test when I get back?" This is a question I had posed to my high school science teacher one year.

My teacher looked me straight in the eye and said, "Your job is to be a student, not to be doing science fairs. It's not right for you to miss school in order to go to science fairs."

I stood there with my mouth open, unable to fathom what this teacher, who I admired until that day, had just told me.

This teacher had no problem moving tests for the athletes in the class. He didn't blink twice when soccer, football, volleyball and track players asked for time off for a game or tournament. This teacher himself was absent frequently supervising or coaching athletic extracurricular activities.

So, why was my request so outlandish? I was representing my school, my town, and my county at the national science fair. This teacher was happy to take the credit when my name appeared in national newspapers, magazines, radio and national television but couldn't support me during the journey because his idea of a "good student" was one who followed the norm and participated in activities that he saw as important. He couldn't imagine or wasn't willing to see the value in science fair competitions.

This incident reflected back to me that I was not good enough. I would only get respect if I fit the mould. I spent most of my upbringing committed to music, dance and science fair competitions—things that I now see reflected my authentic self. But I grew up not feeling good enough, in part because I wasn't good at sports.

Years later, I look back on those conversations with that teacher and the feelings of inadequacy I felt during my high school years and can only laugh. My creative talents and my success in science fairs are what led to my successful career, not my high school science or other course marks. In fact, you can find in my high school right now Grade 10 McGraw Hill textbooks with a written feature on me and my successes.

THE MISFIT

I grew up in a small rural town in Canada with a population of less than 4000. It was incredibly hard to fit in while growing up as a child of immigrant parents in a predominantly White town.

I always felt like I could never win. Do I act like the kids in school and fit in but disappoint my immigrant parents? Do I behave as my parents want me to but stick out like a sore thumb at school?

Trying to create an identity meeting both criteria felt impossible and resulted in a childhood full of loneliness and being bullied.

One memory etched in my heart exemplifies exactly how I felt growing up. It involves me collapsing on the cold hard floor of the girls' bathroom in the fetal position, crying, feeling helpless, feeling unwanted and feeling not good enough.

I was attending a grade school dance, initially feeling excited and nervous because I absolutely loved dancing but I knew I didn't have any friends.

I had no one to dance with. I remember going around trying to dance around groups of people. Around one group, they looked back at me and said "hold on a second." They then huddled together, reviewed the matter and turned back to say "we discussed it, and you can't dance with us." This type of rejection happened over and over again.

I can still feel the utter humiliation of being turned away so many times. I didn't know what else to do because I couldn't leave since the dance was happening during school hours. That was how I ended up on the bathroom floor in the fetal position, crying, feeling helpless, feeling unwanted and feeling not good enough.

During my childhood, I never quite fit in because I was always trying to be someone I was not.

So, again, I ask the question, who was I really? I was a loving girl who cared about others and would give the clothes off her back if someone needed it. I had a generous heart and loved music and dancing. I also felt very deeply and was sensitive. I was a Canadian-born Indian girl living in two worlds just trying to have good friends and be a good friend. All I wanted was to be accepted as me.

THE COST OF INAUTHENTICITY

"Who the heck do you think you are?" This was the voice inside my head.

By the age of 20, I had won Canada's Top 20 Under 20. By age 21, I was named "Young Achiever of the Year" by the Indo Canada Chamber of Commerce and had been invited to be the keynote speaker at the prestigious Economic Developers Council Of Ontario annual conference. Media outlets were calling, and I was getting offers from investors to help me commercialize my water technology.

Everyone was telling me how amazing I was. Frankly, I should have been on top of the world, but in truth, I was scared out of my mind. At just barely 21, I had found success but was scared to lose it all. I was afraid of the pure humiliation of failing in front of so many people, and to be honest, I felt completely numb. I didn't know what to do. I had many opportunities right at my fingertips but couldn't make any decisions. I left millions of dollars on the table, all because I felt like an IMPOSTER.

This is what happens when you abandon yourself and become someone you are not. How could I believe in myself if I didn't even know who I was? And so began my journey of finding myself. I am not going to lie to you; it's been full of ups and downs.

The truth is that if we let it, our subconscious mind runs the show. 95% of what we do every single day is controlled by our subconscious mind. Would you believe that the majority of our subconscious programming happens by the time we turn 7? In my case, clearly, I had a lot of conditioning to undo.

Fast forward to today, I am devoted to authenticity. I strive daily to show up authentically as who I am because I intimately understand the cost of inauthenticity. For me, the cost was self-doubt, loneliness, lost time and millions of dollars left behind. But I wouldn't change the past because it is what has got me to where I currently stand.

Today, I run three successful businesses that fuel my soul.

Water Technology Company. I am currently commercializing a patented solar desalination technology. I invented this environmentally friendly water purification technology that uses only the sun and seawater, with no external energy required. This technology can be applied in industrial, residential and agricultural settings.

Water Well-ness Project. We are a philanthropic organization focused on water, sanitation and hygiene challenges worldwide. Entrepreneurs can invest in projects that provide an opportunity to do social good and make a financial return at the same time.

Asha Suppiah International. I help feminine-leaning entrepreneurs to lead authentically, as their feminine selves, instead of hustling, controlling and straining their way to the top.

I am proud to be using all that I have learned growing my businesses to now help other feminine-leaning entrepreneurs to avoid the mistakes I faced. I am here to show women how they can be themselves even when the whole world is pressuring them to be someone else.

I was told who to be my entire life and frankly, I became sick and tired of people telling me who to be.

For example:

- Parents telling me who to be
- Indian society telling me who to be
- Canadian culture telling me who to be
- Television shows telling me who to be
- Peers telling me who to be
- Teachers telling me who to be
- Industry leaders and peers telling me who to be

What I've shared in this chapter is my true story showing how we can't fake our way to happiness and success. The bottom line is that the pursuit to meet society's expectations is a fool's errand and a special sort of pain. It requires you to live in misery trying to meet everyone's expectations while secretly knowing on the inside that you will never truly meet their expectations. It took me decades to realize I was putting myself through all this pain without reason. I wasn't getting the success I wanted, I didn't have the friends I wanted and I wasn't happy. Trust me, I fell off the path of authenticity a few times over my career and every single time it caught up with me.

SLIDING BACK TO OLD PATTERNS

After seeing success in my other businesses, I decided to enter the online coaching/consulting industry. I wanted to teach others what I had learned growing my other two businesses but had no clue how the online coaching world worked. So, I hired my first coach and began listening to online coaching gurus. So began my journey of losing myself for a number of years. I spent thousands of dollars on coaches, consultants and mentors, with everyone continually guiding me in divergent directions. I was told to be a high-performance coach, then told to switch to a success coach, then a mindset coach, then a money mindset coach, then a sales coach. Each expert I hired claimed that the reason I wasn't seeing the epic level of success I wanted was that I was coaching the wrong subject. Or, they claimed that I needed to use their strategy to succeed. Each coach told me their strategy was better than the last coach I had hired.

I was getting pulled further and further away from my true authentic self. I started to believe these ideas that were being shared with me and kept changing the direction of my business and my strategy over and over again. I was struggling for the first couple of years in business and I had no clue why since I was hiring coach after coach and was not afraid to invest money into my business. In complete frustration, I brought this question into my mediation practice and asked the universe "what am I doing wrong" and the answer I got was crystal clear: I was not running my business authentically.

I only began to see true success in my online coaching/consulting business when I started to show up as my true authentic self, not the manufactured identity the coaches I was hiring were pushing on me. And it's like "Well, duh, authenticity is what brought you success in your other businesses." Sometimes we have to learn the lesson over and over again.

"Authenticity is a collection of choices that we have to make every day. It's about the choice to show up and be real. The choice to be honest. The choice to let our true selves be seen." - Brené Brown

Here's my truth: The fastest path to success and happiness is through authenticity. Authenticity means being yourself no matter what anyone else says. It means honouring who you are inside, regardless of what society dictates. Authenticity is about respecting yourself enough to know that you are ENOUGH.

Time is here for *the authentic woman*.

THE AUTHENTIC WOMAN

This is the day we come out of hiding
This is the day we own our truth.
This is the day we claim our POWER.
We are not the chains that hold us back.
The authentic woman is here to change the world
She is here to make the world a more fair, just, and loving place.
She is here to HEAL the world.
She is reclaiming her worthiness.
She is reclaiming her voice.
She is reclaiming her SELF.
She steps into her center so she can change the world.
She transforms the world while becoming unapologetically rich.
She uses her money to elevate herself and the world around her.
My greatest wish for you is that you bravely step into your authenticity and take back your life.

ABOUT THE AUTHOR

Asha Suppiah is an award-winning serial entrepreneur who has been making a name for herself in male-dominant industries for over 20 years. She is the go-to feminine leadership expert and works with high-achieving female entrepreneurs who want to carve out their market position as industry leaders but don't want to hustle, wrestle, and control their way to the top.

Asha helps feminine-leaning entrepreneurs to lead authentically, as their feminine selves, instead of partaking in the prescribed masculine form of leadership. She is passionate about re-defining leadership and ushering in a new Feminine Leadership Revolution where feminine qualities like intuition, kindness, vulnerability and collaboration are celebrated not shunned.

Website: www.ashasuppiah.com
Email: hello@ashasuppiah.com
Facebook: www.facebook.com/ashasuppiah
Instagram: www.instagram.com/ashasuppiah

4

BRAD WALSH

This is the story of my upbringing that eventually, many years later, led me on my journey into the world of Women's Empowerment.

Hello. My name is Bradley Edward Walsh. I was born on February 6th, 1970. My given name was Bradley John Edward Sibbitt. I was born to Brenda Mary Walsh and John Homer Sibbitt in East York General Hospital in Toronto, Ontario Canada, and a two and a half years later, became a big brother to Jason Lee Sibbitt.

According to my mother, I was in and out of the hospital or basically spent the first 5 years of my life in Toronto Sick Kids Hospital. I really don't remember very much, if any of that time. I do, however, remember having severe nose bleeds to the point where I had lost so much blood multiple times and they didn't know if I was going to survive. I had so many blood transfusions and nose cauterizations as a result of all the blood loss.

After coming out on the other side of those personal health struggles as a child, for the most part, I was a pretty happy kid growing up and led a pretty normal life as far as lives go for children. I received lots of love and support from my mom and grandparents (my mom's parents). I had lots of friends and played sports—soccer, in particular, was my sport of choice. I absolutely loved the game. My upbringing was middle class. My mom stayed home with my brother and I to raise us and my father worked at General Motors on the assembly line to bring in the money to support the family.

We ended up moving to Oshawa, Ontario, because it was closer to my father's workplace. I must have been about 8 years old at the time and of course that was an adjustment, having to leave all my friends and everything I knew up to that point to move to another city about 30 minutes away. I don't remember a lot of fighting and arguing in the house between my parents growing up but I do remember my dad not being around very much or attending any of my soccer games.

My mom and my nana were always there on the sidelines cheering me on, I remember that. I can remember my mom telling me stories about when the three of us were out together, strangers would think my nana was my mother instead of my mom.

When I was 10, I vividly remember my mother coming to my brother and I and telling us, as gently as a parent could tell my brother and I who were 10 and 8 years old at the time that she and my father were going to be splitting up but they still both loved us very much, and that it had nothing to do with Jay and I; it wasn't our fault—they just decided it was time to go their own way, or something to that effect. I can remember at first being kind of shocked and upset and wondering why. Lots of questions ran through my head and of course my parents always told us, we understand this is a big adjustment and we understand you will have questions so just know you can come to us and we will do our best to answer them for you. My brother and I were both asked and given the choice of which parent we wanted to live with. Of course as young boys, we chose to live with our mother as I am sure most young boys around that age would probably choose as well, given the option.

I'm not going to lie to you, the adjustment period was a little rough as to be expected but nothing too horrible where I was acting out or being a terrible child and disrespectful to my parents as a result of it. I just kind of adapted to the "new norm" as it were and accepted what was happening. It just meant that my parents weren't going to be living in the same house, I would now at the tender young age of 10 have to step up and become the "man" of the house (at least in my mind) and I would have to go spend every other weekend with my father at his house and then come back to Mom's house on Sunday nights. At that age, I didn't have a lot of friends that had divorced or separated parents so that was a little bit different and something to get used to but really unaffected by it for the most part.

So, my mom, my brother, and I ended up moving across the street from the townhouse complex where we used to live with both of my parents, into an apartment building where my grandparents lived. This was obviously partially a bit of luck that an apartment was available in that building and of course convenience and help for my now newly single parent mother.

The every-other-weekend visitations weren't really fulfilling me or giving me what I needed; I felt myself as time went on in that first year not really wanting to go and spend time with my father or even missing him for that matter when I wasn't with him. I just wanted to be back at Mom's house (home) to hang out with my friends and spend time with Mom. By the age of 12, apparently according to the law, I was old enough to decide for myself if I wanted to continue on seeing my father every other weekend as appointed by the court. I decided it wasn't something I wanted to continue doing, and so I stopped altogether. This of course upset him and unfortunately my brother still had to legally go for his visitation weekends so I would periodically see my father when he came to pick my brother up and drop him off from his weekend visits and that was about the extent of it.

As my brother came of the legal age to make that decision for himself, he too decided to follow in my footsteps and not continue with the visitation weekends. This of course upset my father even more but my mother was very supportive of our choice and always reassured us that at any time, we could absolutely go and see him, it was up to us. She wasn't going to be one of those parents that stood in the way of her children spending time with their father. Both my brother and I decided to stick to our guns and stay with our original decision. This of course created a rift and caused extreme strain on my relationship with my father, but to be honest, I really wasn't bothered by it. Even when he was in the picture, he was never really around or much of a father to me anyway, so in mind even at that young age, I knew this was the best decision for me.

Those years from the age 11 well into my teens were especially formative for me because I not only strengthened my relationship with my mother as a result of the situation we were now in but I also established a much stronger bond with my nana due to the amount of time we were spending together and bonding through. I believe those years definitely played an integral part in making me the man I am today, and I have those two women in my life to thank for that. They were the foundation for all of it, for all that I am today. There truly aren't enough words in the English language to express my gratitude for my mom and my nana. They taught me so much during that time in my life and yes the obvious stuff that parents and grandparents teach their kids and grandkids but I think it was more the unspoken lessons of doing what needed to be done and leading by example not only as a parent and grandparent but as phenomenally strong women, each in their own right. What they taught me unknowingly had an even greater impact on me and helped shape who I am today and for that I am forever grateful and forever in their debt, for those invaluable lessons.

We ended up leaving Oshawa when I was about 14 or so and ended up moving back to our old neighbourhood in Toronto, and I was reunited with all my old friends and familiar faces. It felt great to be back. Although it was great to be back, I must say, I did truly miss the closeness I had with my nana and how much closer we had grown while we had that time to spend together and bond. I adjusted pretty quickly and got back into the swing of things and made new friends as we do when we enter a new school. It wasn't easy but who says being a teen is easy, right?

During my later teen years, Mom met a man she liked and ended up falling in love with and getting together with. Now as a teenager who had been used to being the "man" of the house, now having to concede that responsibility so to speak was a little difficult. That period in "our" lives was not without its challenges, and I do realize now that those challenges and the cause of, could greatly be contributed to me being difficult, pushing the boundaries to see how far I could push them. I made things quite rough for my mother and the new man in her life at times but we did get through it all and came out the other side much better for it. Over time I came to love this man as a father and even started calling him Dad. He was an incredible man who cared and loved my mom deeply and in turn, he loved my brother and I like his own children, even though he had children of his own from a previous marriage. This man I now called Dad taught me and brought so much to my life, so much I didn't even know was missing really, even though I never had a father figure around. I can tell you that I looked at this man as more of a father to me than my biological father ever was and that filled my heart. He actually took the time to teach, share and instill values that a father should do for his children. This man completely changed my life. He is the third person in my life that I am truly grateful and forever indebted to. He was also of paramount importance in helping to form and create the human, the man I am today.

When I was in high school, I found my first love, my first passion and no it wasn't a girl, it was photography. Now keep in mind, back in those days, photographs were created or made with film cameras. It's a totally different ball game compared to the digital age we are in now. I took a photography class and fell in love. I loved the creative process and seeing the images come to life before my very eyes on that piece of photography paper. I loved the smell of the chemicals, the process, everything about it —I was hooked.

Once I left high school, sure I would have loved to be a photographer but that was unrealistic, you certainly can't make money as an artist and other than that I had no idea what I wanted to do with my life, where I wanted to go or who I wanted to be. I figured well I might as well get a job while I think about it and figure it out so I did exactly that. I worked for about 5 years before deciding I wanted to go off to college to study Audio-Visual Techniques, which translates to audio production, television production, editing and of course photography. I absolutely loved those 2 years of college, got my diploma and here I was again, ok what can I do with this, where do I go with this piece of paper?

I ended up getting a job in my field of expertise and enjoyed it. The job afforded me a lot of great luxuries. I got to travel all over North America on the company dime, which was great, I met a lot of wonderful people, forged some great friendships that I still have to this day but something was missing, I just didn't know what at the time. I ended up moving into a corporate role within a large globally known accounting firm in their audio-visual department. I finally felt like I had arrived. I was making more money than I had ever made; I was putting my hard-earned college diploma to work by finding a job within the corporate world that was also in my field of expertise. It was great, what did I have to complain about right? Well, if truth be told, nothing at least not for the first 5 or 6 years of my tenure at the company which I ended up staying at for a total of 12 and a half years.

Those last 6 years of my corporate career were absolutely miserable. I woke up every morning dreading having to go to work. I hated my job. I was empty inside but kept pushing through anyway because I didn't think or know any different for myself. A couple of positive things that came from that whole experience were, number one, I fell in love with corporate headshot photography, which I never ever thought would happen because photographing humans was never something I wanted. Secondly, I realize and woke up to the fact that life doesn't have to be like this, there is much more to it than the corporate life and making a comfortable living and having the benefits and all the perks of a "comfortable corporate job."

In the middle of this whole self-discovery or self-realization phase of my journey, I met the love of my life, my now wife Mary, while out with some friends one night. Our relationship blossomed over the next few years into something beautiful. Mary had children from a previous marriage, two beautiful little girls who were aged 4 and 6 when I came into the picture. As my relationship with Mary grew stronger, so did my relationship with those two beautiful little girls, Nicole and Julia. I loved them dearly and like my father before me did with my brother and I, I took those two girls on as my very own children, even though I was not their birth father. I did all the things and took on all the responsibilities as if I were because I loved them and Mary that much. We got married 7 years into our relationship and Mary and the rest as they say is history. That's not to say that our relationship hasn't had its shares of ups and downs as does every relationship by all in all, we have each other's backs and that's what matters when all is said and done.

After speaking with Mary about it, and having her get on board with my idea and plan, I decided in that last half of my corporate career that I was going to finally try to give this photography business idea a shot. I finally left my corporate job after 12 and a half years of safety and security and let me tell you, as any entrepreneur will tell you, it was scary as all hell. My entrepreneurial journey has been one hell of a windy road, and it has taken me places I never ever thought I would end up or go. My entrepreneurial adventure as a photographer has had many stops and detours along the way. I started out shooting architecture and landscapes, creating my art and exhibiting and selling my art at local art shows around Toronto. This then progressed into doing corporate and actor headshots which then turned into me really starting my journey into women's empowerment and women's empowerment photography or what is better known as Boudoir Photography.

Two and a half years into my life as a full time photographer, my whole business and life as I knew it was turned upside down and forever altered—hell the whole world experienced something we had never ever seen in our lifetime and probably never will again. We were hit with a global pandemic which in itself is a massive shift for everyone around the world. It basically rendered my photography business inoperable. I guess you could call it divine timing if that's your thing but the universe clearly had other plans for me for this next chapter of my life.

I obviously had to adapt, shift, and do something quickly as we all did in the entrepreneurial world, but what was I going to do?

I got tired of hearing all the negativity and complaining and whining and bitching about the current situation in the world, and I immediately decided that that wasn't for me. I wasn't going to feed into it.

I had wanted to start a podcast for quite some time but just never got around to it due to imposter syndrome, lack of time and I guess sheer laziness. Well, here was my shining moment, my golden opportunity to make it happen for myself. I decided that I would do something positive in the face of negativity with all that was going on and start my very own podcast. I figured why not take what I was doing with the Women's

Empowerment Photography and take the principles and values of that and turn it into a podcast that focuses solely on women. I wanted to provide a space that highlighted and elevated women, that amplified women's voices and what better platform to do that with than a podcast.

Little did I know that all those unspoken lessons and moments that my mom and my nana instilled in me, unbeknownst to them, would inspire and turn me into a Women's Empowerment Advocate. Those two women who were the foundation for all of this, along with my wife, Mary, and my two daughters Nicole and Julie, are entirely, singlehandedly instrumental and inspirational in bringing the Empowerography Platform to life. I would like to thank those five women for all that they have taught me, shown me and brought to my life. I owe you all so very much. You all had a hand in transforming me into the man I am today.

ABOUT THE AUTHOR

Brad Walsh is a father to two beautiful girls aged 21 and 23, husband to an amazingly inspiring woman, photographer, and podcast host/producer who found himself wanting to inspire others during the pandemic. He birthed the idea of EMPOWEROGRAPHY as a platform to highlight strong, inspired and dynamic women to share their stories of success triumph, resiliency and transformation. He had no idea that what started as a simple concept would take on a life of its own. He is so excited to share this platform with you and continue to EMPOWER, ELEVATE, and EDUCATE by amplifying the voices of women all over the world. So please join him in spreading the word about his mission/collective/movement he us creating to provide a platform for women to empower and inspire other women out there in the world.

Website: www.empowerographypodcast.com
Instagram: www.instagram.com/empowerographypodcast
Email: empowerographypodcast@gmail.com

5

BRIGID HOLDER

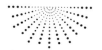

LIGHTING UP MY LIFE

Sometimes in life, you never know which seeds out of the many you plant will sprout and take your breath away.

In my mid-forties, when everything seemed to be in place; husband, career and kids, I felt restless. I needed to find something else to light me up, maybe even a few small things that could add up to meaning and purpose.

Leaving behind my big corporate job as second-in-command of a major shipping organisation, I started a business with my husband. That felt better, but only for a short while. I still needed something else for myself, so I started working in one and then a second MLM company on the side. The second became a quick success but didn't sit right with my desire to do more, be more, aim higher, leave a legacy in this world beyond my offspring. Stumbling around like a woman wearing a sleep-mask, I grasped at other things I thought would spark joy. I ran a mother's mentorship program, then partnered with a friend to uplift women, and even went into business mentoring. I was good—even great—at all these yet still yearned for something more. Nothing lit that fire or felt even close to my own slice of Heaven on Earth. After I wrote a chapter in my first multi-author book, it was like someone ripped off the mask, let the light peek in, and I could finally feel this was the beginning of an incredible journey being laid out before me.

From the moment I put my pen to paper, storytelling became a part of me and still is the most profound part of my life's work right now. Did I know this would happen as I sat down to vent and call bullshit on the societal expectations around Motherhood? Of course not. Did I know that one day I would be the one publishing women's stories with my own publishing house? Hell no; that was a universal delivery yet to come. I was simply learning to follow, chase, and plant experiences in my life that made me feel alive.

The truth and vulnerability in my short story prompted many women to reach out. They thanked me for speaking their thoughts out loud. They told me they no longer felt alone. Some of them said I gave them permission to feel their feelings without judgement. Others were able to speak their truth for the very first time. Ah, now this felt more like it!

"When you find your light, you shine from the inside and it is felt externally."

BLOOM WHERE YOU'RE PLANTED? OR MOVE TOWARD THE SUN?

A change started blossoming in me. I wanted to offer more to women and to the world. I had to learn a few things that would teach me how to do that. Like when it comes to making any decision, not just the important ones, I need to stop looking outside myself. It's important to close my eyes and ears, to stop listening to what other people say or think. Now I know that anything less than a full-body yes is an absolute nope, not for me.

Following the vines of my newest seedling, I started to grow beyond my comfort zone. This is a critical lesson because the growing process teaches us the most. You can compare it to climbing a mountain; the obstacles and challenges along the way are what the journey is all about. Getting to the destination or reaching that summit is far less important. And if you think about it, the person who arrives at that summit will undoubtedly be a different person than the one who started the climb.

Sure, there are obstacles, but in a stormy wind, you'll develop stronger roots. And if we take this back to my seed/plant metaphor, you might not even make it all the way up the mountain before you find the place you are meant to plant yourself. Aim for that summit, sure, but stay focused on each step in the present moment so we can reach much more soul-focused goals. Having that inner game sorted is far more important and beneficial to your own self than any summit will be.

"Choose to move toward the sun whilst you bloom in the place you were planted!"

A BEGINNER'S MIND. WHO DO YOU WANT TO BE?

As we grow up, particularly in teenage years (and I am witnessing this with my growing teens), we are asked, "What do you want to do when you leave school?" or "What do you want to do when you grow up?" We admire the little ones for saying a policeman, fire man or astronaut. We read them stories about different jobs they might chose when they are adults. I'm sure my kids are used to hearing this question now because people have been asking them some form of it since they were young children, just as I was, just as you were.

A better question we should be asking our young people (and ourselves) is:

Who do you want to become?

What a grander and more expansive question about who they are inside! About their humanity! We are not what we do; we are WHO WE ARE. Should we not teach children this is infinitely more important than a job title?

And I'll throw another twist on it, just to blow your mind a little more. We should also tell young people (and ourselves) that IT'S OKAY NOT TO KNOW. Insert shocked emoji face. Maybe they know, maybe they don't. Maybe they (and we) get to decide who we want to become for ourselves. I know this concept made me uncomfortable for a long time. The audacity that I could actually choose who I wanted to be! We are conditioned to plan our lives according to norms and forget to dream about who we want to become.

Over the last few years, I have faced this wild question head-on. Who do I want to BE? It comes up a lot in our home, so it seems my boys and I are learning life's lessons at the same time. I started by making a list. For your homework, I recommend you make one, too. Don't compare it to mine, don't assume or make judgements that mine is better than yours or vice versa; just write the list and watch what comes next!

"Choose to be who you want, not what others want of you."

WHO I WANT TO BE. MY LIST.

- I want to be the leader of a movement allowing women to express themselves in a way that lights them and their readers or listeners up from the inside.
- I want to be the woman who grants another woman permission to change perspective on her current reality through my stories.
- I want to be a catalyst for change, the permission slip another woman needs to create a new, better life for herself.
- I want to stand up and speak up for those who are too afraid to speak.
- I want to talk about the topics that people are afraid to talk about.
- I want to be fit and healthy as I age, valuing my mind and body —the one they say 'she is incredible,' at 60, at 70 at 80, at 90 at 100!
- I want to be the mother who allows her children the freedom to become the men they wish to be, to be present when they need me and to show them by example.

This all-encompassing question, 'Who do I want to be'? took me on a ride I didn't particularly feel like going on. I dove into deep waters and swam far outside my comfort zone. I had to show up for myself when things felt too hard and stick to my commitment to help others, especially when I felt depleted. I even had to face some childhood fears instead of ignoring them forevermore. If I had not done this work, I might be living with that sleeping mask on again and with that unsettled feeling of life living me, not the other way around. I certainly would not be where I am now.

The summit can be reached as long as we are willing to let the lessons along the way land with us and actually learn from them. Know your own worth and power to achieve anything you set your hearts desire to do!

"Find your own summit, conquer it and grow on the way."

WHERE AM I NOW? HERE, OF COURSE.

Today, I am a publisher of women's stories. I set the business up alone, but I shall never do it alone—collaboration and community also lights me up. I enable women to experience that same impact on others that I humbly had with my first published chapter. I cast a vision and grant them owner-ship of this. By giving women a platform to share, they can also experi-ence that same gift and use it to redesign their lives. This is how I can magnify my own little slice of Heaven on Earth and make sure more people get to experience it as I have. The ripple effect again enhancing my life and theirs.

I am surrounded now, by the most incredible angels, from my VA in the Philippines, my IT guru in Perth, my all-rounder and podcast queen Florida Belle, an editor in Sydney and an editor and extremely talented artist in Melbourne, plus numerous publishers worldwide (geniuses), and the woman who started it all: our publisher of this precious piece of work. I have not yet met all of these women in person, but one day I plan to. This heavenly network catches me if I stumble, gives support and encour-agement when I need it, and they help me to create my soul-on-fire work, which in turn helps countless other women—a beautiful, Earthly cycle.

Going after what lights you up is not selfish; it's a duty. It is what you were put here to do and you simply must do it.

This work impacts your children if you have them or other young people watching. When you give your gifts to the world, you affect your entire circle, the ripple effect is real. I encourage you then to take my advice and step into your desires; allow this to be the winning code for you, your family and your community.

"Create the community you crave to enable the collaborations to light you up!"

WHERE TO FROM HERE? THE ALL-IMPORTANT 'NOW WHAT'?

Tricked you. We're going to stop being so goal-focused, remember? That way, we don't ever have to ask, "Now What?" ever again. We can live in the present moment and understand that the only constant in life is change. The sooner we embrace impermanence, the sooner we can feel more content in our lives and more hopeful about our futures.

I want us all to see what is possible by climbing our own mountains, growing beyond our containers, and finding that ease and grace in life. I know this is possible because I've found it! You do have to be willing to keep growing and stretching. I won't stop until I'm dead, but I live every day knowing that I'm doing my best work. Living my best life, you can choose this too! It was not until my late forties I found my passion and it might evolve, it might completely change and that's ok. It is ok and it is welcomed!

Do not stop searching for what lights you up, your passion, what brings you joy, for at the end of the search there is your slice of heaven of earth included in that is your community, great communication and many collaborations for you to continue to grow and learn through.

Remember when I told you that to decide to do something, it needs to be a full-body yes? That's what purpose feels like. It also feels like every morning when I jump out of bed, excited to take on the day. And that's what it feels like when I fall asleep at night, knowing I've done some good that day. I think you deserve that too. Catch that vision, drive yourself forward and until you truly and whole heartedly believe in yourself, surround yourself (like I have done) with women who believe in you.

I look forward to reading your chapter in a multi-author book and hearing how you leaned in on this ever-evolving journey we call life!

"You too deserve your best life!"
B xx

ABOUT THE AUTHOR

Seven times International Best-Selling Publisher and USA Today Best Selling Author, Brigid Holder of The Art of Grace Publishing House, loves to push the boundaries of publishing. Her literary prose spotlights empowerment, truth telling, and women breaking barriers. She believes that stories have the power to impact and shift multi-generational patterns. Her goal is collaborate with others in leaving a legacy that evokes heartfelt wisdom and to honours bad-ass heroines, all the while cultivating a blazing literary trail for emerging authors to follow. Most recently, a new collaboration digital magazine, *The Journey of Words*, is shining a light on all things writing and publishing for our entrepreneurial publishing industry. When she is not publishing, Brigid can be found hiking and at her boys' sporting meets, fostering her own empowerment, and watching her family create lasting memories, surely to later be found bound by a curated collection of words.

Website: *www.brigidholder.com*

6

DEREK ALVAREZ

I usually do the formatting/typesetting here at AMA Publishing and as I was doing my thing, I was inspired and felt like I have something to contribute to the theme of this book. When it comes to the subject of "Sacred Redesign," I've often felt that I've gone through many transformations throughout my life, although I'm not so sure they have all been "sacred."

Early on in my life, my environment forced me to be tougher than I naturally am. Naturally, I am pretty sensitive. Growing up where I did, in San Bernardino, California, I had to adapt and develop much thicker skin. In San Bernardino, I was an oddity. I was a blonde-haired, blue-eyed boy in an area where it was more common to have brown or black skin. Even though I had many friends who didn't look like me, I often experienced racism from both peers and adults.

Art was always an escape for me, and I would often doodle in class. One day, in my 4th-grade class, I was doodling and not really paying attention to the teacher. No teacher likes this, of course, but this teacher—an African-American—took it upon himself to grab my drawing, crumble it up, and tell the class that despite this behavior, I would one day be their boss because of my skin color.

It was difficult to like myself in this environment. An honor-roll student through 6th-grade, I got my first "F" in 7th grade. I didn't fit in, and I couldn't focus on school with all the noise I was surrounded by.

The subtitle of this book contains the phrase, "how to free yourself from society's standards." The truth is, I never had to free myself, because it was impossible to conform when the standard was something I had no control over—my skin color.

It pains me to see that this narrative has entered the mainstream in my country. If you are a white male, you are considered evil incarnate.

Dr. Martin Luther King said in his famous "I Have a Dream" speech: *"I have a dream that my four little children will one day live in a nation where they will not be judged by the color of their skin but by the content of their character."*

In the US, we have a national holiday celebrating this man, and rightfully so. But unless we apply his dream to everyone, the dream is dead.

MY FIRST HINT AT A LARGER WORLD

My first hint that things might be different elsewhere came about through travel. A few times in my youth, we would go to Mexico, where some of my stepdad's family lives. Mexico is of course plagued with many of the same issues I grew up with in San Bernardino—but is also quite different than what I grew up with, as well.

In Mexico, I experienced a culture that values family—and often has so much fun and zest for life—despite not being what most Americans would consider "wealthy," monetarily speaking. I've found Mexicans to be very warm and very easy to make friends with. Sure, I would see poverty that was often worse than what I would see in my neighborhood, but I've observed that some of the poorest people in the world are also some of the happiest. It doesn't make sense to most Westerners, but there can be great joy in living simply.

Sometimes we would visit Nogales, Arizona, too. My stepdad would take us to his grandpa's house. He didn't speak a word of English, but my stepdad would translate for us. He would tell us stories of how Pancho Villa came to town when he was a boy because he was looking for young kids to add to his gang. (His mother hid him and saved him from a violent future.)

He lived very simply in a small house, with chickens in his backyard. Every meal I ever had with him consisted of beans, tortillas, and eggs—fresh from his flock. He was one of the happiest people I've ever met—always with a smile on his face and a joke ready.

CULTURE SHOCK

When I was about 15, my parents decided they had enough of San Bernardino. So, they did some research and decided to move to North Dakota, which had the least crime of any state in the US at that time.

Oddly enough, I wasn't excited about this move. I lived in a violent, crime-infested shithole, but I was a teenager, and I had friends I had known for 10 years. Most of my friends smoked marijuana, some were in gangs, and some were on their way to jail—but you never have friends quite like you do when you were a kid. Now that I'm 41, I realize that more than ever. The bonds you make from knowing kids from age 6 on, you just can't re-create.

Ironically, my skin color fit right in with the majority of North Dakotans, but culturally, we were miles apart. (Try a little experiment and tell someone in small-town or rural America that you're from California, and see how it goes.)

Looking back, there were some amazing things about North Dakota in the late 90's that you just don't find many places today. The people were friendly, they would make sure to say hello, and they would help dig your car out of the snow after a blizzard. You could go to the market in the winter and leave your car running without worrying about it getting stolen. It was so vastly different from my upbringing, and their way of life was something I didn't even know existed.

Ultimately, it was the winter that drove us off. Winters in North Dakota are brutal—they measure snow in feet, not inches. The land is flat, and it's hard to see the horizon in all the gray. The day we packed our U-Haul and headed out, the temperature was -60 degrees Fahrenheit, with the windchill. I think we lasted about 9 months in North Dakota.

My parents decided to move to Tucson, Arizona instead. The difference in the weather is about as opposite as you can get—people seek

Arizona out in the winter because it is so mild. Most of the rest of the year is brutally hot, of course.

Tucson was a great fit for me. Although it was growing substantially, it had a small-town vibe. The problems I grew up with in San Bernardino were not nearly as prevalent in "The Old Pueblo." There are a lot of Mexican-Americans and a lot of white people, and they all get along quite nicely, for the most part.

MY FIRST POSITIVE REDESIGN

Until age 15, I grew up in ignorance—surrounded by poverty, hatred, drug abuse, homelessness, violence. I got in so many fights in elementary school that I had my own tree I had to stand by at recess, where I would be in eyesight of the school principal.

My first awakening, and "redesign" came when I went to college. Because I let my grades slip in junior high and high school, the best I could do was community college. I had no plan or thoughts for the future. My mom told me I'd better get a job or go to college, so I chose college. Being treated like an adult invigorated me—I chose my schedule and my classes, and I was motivated to get good grades again, partly because I was now paying for it, and also because I was interested in what I was learning.

One of my elective classes was art. I rediscovered my passion for it, and also realized I was pretty good at it. One day, we got to take a field trip to the University of Arizona School of Art. I met a painting teacher named Alfred Quiroz, a bit of an eccentric, who I instantly hit it off with. He became a mentor and even helped me get a scholarship that covered half of my tuition. The other half, I paid off with part-time jobs. (I am lucky to have graduated college without any student-loan debt.)

I majored in Fine Arts—specifically, oil painting. I thrived because I was extremely interested in what I was learning.

In the arts, it is inevitable you will come across gay people. Growing up in San Bernardino, we were extremely macho and homophobic. We would call each other "gay" or a "fag" to put each other down. We would even play a game called "Smear the Queer"—a free-for-all where anyone who had possession of the football would get tackled by the rest of the kids. The boys in my neighborhood would talk about beating up anyone who acted "gay" in their presence. This was my upbringing.

College changed my perspective. It opened me up to different perspectives and ways of life. I made friends with a gay guy. It was the best thing I ever did, because he introduced me to my wife, Adriana—my soul-mate and my business partner.

I also started to read a lot in college. I decided to read the classics, the books considered the greatest in literature—books like Moby Dick, Great Expectations, War and Peace, Crime and Punishment, The Brothers Karamazov, Les Misérables, The Sound and The Fury, and on and on. I also read some modern classics, like Cold Mountain, Fahrenheit 451, Rabbit Run, One Flew Over the Cuckoo's Nest, All The President's Men, The Great Gatsby, etc.

Nowadays, I am surrounded by entrepreneurs who mostly read self-help and non-fiction, but fiction has taught me a lot. It helped me understand other points of view and to realize I am not alone in many of my thoughts and feelings. It opened me up to a whole new world that I was previously unaware of.

MY SECOND POSITIVE REDESIGN

After college, I continued to paint. I sold my paintings at a gallery on Marshall Way in Scottsdale, Arizona. I also worked as a waiter, to fill in my income gaps. Adriana still chose to marry me in this situation. We married on 7/7/07.

After we married, I decided I'd better get a better paying job. I applied for a job as a landscape designer with a big landscaping company in Tucson, despite not feeling qualified, since my degree was in Fine Arts—not Landscape Design. I interviewed well and landed the job. I picked it up quickly and had a great time doing it, too. Until the real estate bubble burst in 2008.

Going to work everyday became very stressful. So much so that I would often enter the office with a pounding headache. My co-workers were being laid off left and right. People I had become friends with were no longer employed. People with families and children to take care of. The final straw came when one of the owners of the company (it was owned by 2 brothers) decided to take an extravagant hunting trip to Africa in the middle of all this. He came back and shared photos of the exotic animals he and his sons had killed—crocodiles, baboons, antelopes. Everyone knew he had spent a small fortune on this. Yet, he kept laying people off.

I had had enough. Adriana encouraged me to quit and start a business in the middle of this economic crisis. It sounded like a crazy idea at the time.

I would need to transform from employee to entrepreneur. Without much capital to start with, we decided to join a multi-level marketing company. We did okay, but it was a steep learning curve. Finances were tight, and we sometimes had a negative balance in our account, which resulted in quite a few overdraft fees.

The best thing about the experience was the self-development. Although network marketing isn't my cup of tea as a business model, I will admit that you can get some of the best leadership and personal development training after you join one. And we did.

I would say the secret to Adriana's and my success in business has been our adaptability. It didn't take long for us to see there was a need among the entrepreneurs we were networking with, and we decided to fill that need.

It all started with us hiring someone to create a website for us. They took way too long and did a mediocre job. I had learned how to create websites in college, so we decided to make that our business. We worked faster than typical web designers, and we differentiated ourselves at the time by also making the websites SEO-friendly.

Soon we took a leap of faith and moved to downtown San Diego, California. We barely had enough money to pay our deposit and first month's rent for our 8th-story loft, but we did it anyway, and trusted ourselves to make it happen.

The move paid off as we were surrounded by more forward-thinking entrepreneurs and business owners who caught the vision of being found near the top of organic Google searches.

The first few months were exciting and fun—we were having a blast as our business skyrocketed and we enjoyed all that living in downtown San Diego had to offer. In the end, we burnt ourselves out with work and the constant party atmosphere of the Gaslamp district. I was regularly working 12-hour days for demanding clients, and Adriana could see that I couldn't keep going on like that.

MY THIRD POSITIVE REDESIGN

Adriana had travelled to many exotic places before we met. She had volunteered to help in places like Burma (now Myanmar), Albania, and Kenya. She would tell me about these places—without omitting the hardships—with a twinkle in her eye. She would tell me about the piles of trash, the power outages, the lack of heating and scarcity of food in Tirana, Albania (post Kosovo Crisis) for example, and tell me how much she missed it there.

I was intrigued. I had to see a place like this—a place with so much going wrong for it—yet a place that was also enjoyed so much that she longed to go back. I guess I could understand because of my experiences in Mexico.

Looking back, I think I made my decision to go for it when we were visiting with some friends we made in San Diego. I sat there and listened to Adriana and a friend of our friend talk about all of their traveling exploits. I thought to myself, "It all sounds so fun and adventurous—I would like to have some of these experiences for myself."

Adriana sealed the deal when she told me, "You need to do more stupid things." So we sold nearly every possession we had and moved to Albania.

I became a traveler. Over the years, we lived or traveled to such places as Greece, Montenegro, Croatia, Bosnia, Costa Rica, up and down Italy—including Sicily (a favorite of mine), and even parts of Mexico I had never been to. We did this for many years—we even had two sons and took them along. (By the way, I came to love Albania, too, but you won't understand unless you go spend some time there yourself.)

MY CURRENT REDESIGN

In 2019, I was ready to come back to the US. I wanted to put down some roots and I thought maybe living in New Orleans would give us the culture and excitement we were used to while also living in our native country.

And I was right, until COVID hit and changed everything. It's a real shame too, because there were parts of New Orleans that were finally thriving after Hurricane Katrina hit way back in 2005. We lived in Uptown, near Magazine Street. We could walk to Whole Foods, which had empty shelves after the lockdowns were announced. Magazine Street was boarded up. The life of this vibrant city was sucked out of it.

We decided to move to Merida, Mexico because they weren't doing lockdowns at the time. Pretty much as soon as we arrived, they started, too. Mexico was unrecognizable—the life was sucked out even there. We called it house arrest—we felt like prisoners. We bought a Nintendo Switch and played old school Super Mario Brothers, we swam in our pool every day, and we did our damndest not to go crazy.

Finally, we felt the best place to live would be near Adriana's family in her small hometown in the "middle-of-nowhere" (as she calls it) Colorado. We kept an eye on the flights going out of Merida. They were constantly being canceled. We decided it would be best to rent a van and go on an epic road trip through most of Mexico—all the way from the Yucatan to southwest Colorado.

We traveled along the coast, we went through the jungle, we went through scenic country that rivaled the views of Tuscany. I never knew some of these parts of Mexico existed. Along the way, our Angels worked overtime keeping us safe and on track. We repeatedly got stopped at checkpoints without problems. We never got stopped by bandits or cops looking for bribes. And we made it out just before the US decided to completely shut the border down.

We couldn't take a vehicle across, so we got help from the locals to carry our bags over a mile-long stretch of road and bridge. When they couldn't go any further, the Border Patrol agents helped us. We were truly blessed every step of the way.

Adriana's grandma had recently passed on, and her dad offered her house as a place to stay while we figured things out. We fell in love with the place—Adriana had so many fond childhood memories—and we decided to buy it from her dad, uncle, and aunt.

This has been the place of my current redesign—I have embraced the situation, the land, and the potential of the property. I have now planted over 20 fruit trees. I have started a garden that we regularly harvest fruit, herbs, and greens from. I have been learning through research, trial and error, of how to grow food. I have become a homesteader.

When I first met Adriana, I told her I wanted to be a hermit in the desert and that I had missed my calling as a farmer. When I was a young kid, I regularly spent time with my great-grandparents, who had moved to California from Oklahoma during the Great Depression. My great-grandpa always had a garden, a compost bin, fish, tortoises, frogs. He kept bees—he even had a barn in his backyard in the middle of the city. I adored him. He always had a smile on his face and was usually whistling. He knew how to enjoy the simple things, just like my Mexican great-grandfather.

Well, I now live in the high desert and I am growing my own food. I recently put together a beehive to harvest our own honey. We have 2 German Shepherds and 6 cats who do a great job keeping the country mice away. We will soon be adding chickens—and if my youngest son has his way—many more animals.

In a world full of turmoil, this is the most content I've ever been. I am teaching my sons about creating compost, planting trees, raising animals, beekeeping… We go rafting on the river, we go swimming in the lake, we are enjoying the simple things.

We homeschool them and we let them do chores that build their confidence. I am grateful that they don't live in an environment like I did growing up. It took many years, but I am now happy with myself, exactly as I am. I have no doubt I am not finished growing, learning, and evolving, but I am happy with who I have become, how I live my life, and how I treat people.

I am surrounded by love and loved-ones, so I would probably call my current redesign "sacred," after all.

ABOUT THE AUTHOR

Derek Alvarez handles most of the behind-the-scenes work at AMA Publishing; which includes managing designers and editors, formatting books, and updating websites. An art lover and trained fine artist; his favorite job is creating the concepts and finalizing the book cover designs, which he takes a lot of pride in. Currently, he's producing 2 adult coloring books that will come out later this year.

Derek grew up in the inner city, but is now a country boy. Some of his favorite current activities are planting trees, kayaking down the Dolores River, and sitting next to an open fire, which he does with is wife, Adriana, and two sons, Sam and Grant.

Website: www.adrianamoniquealvarez.com
Facebook: www.facebook.com/derek.alvarez
Instagram: www.instagram.com/derekalvarezart

7

DINA MARAIS

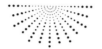

MY JOURNEY HOME

I grew up in a dysfunctional world. When I was born, I would have died had the midwife not injected my heart to jumpstart me back to life. I have often wondered if I didn't try to opt-out of this life, knowing what I signed up for, having already experienced in my mother's womb the violent and traumatic life that lay ahead. I have this visual saying to my Higher Self, "Are you nuts? I'm not right for this?!" And she replied, "You'll be fine, and I'll be there with you all the way."

And so my life began in a family of a 17-year old mother and 22-year old father. My mother was ostracized by the church because she fell pregnant out of wedlock. My father was rejected by his wealthy parents for marrying below their standard. My parents were terrified, with no money to live on. I grew up with this fear of not having money. Not having money meant death!

My mother had four sisters, and they were all beautiful. Let's just say, I was not seen in the same way. Aunt Anna, a neighbour of my grandparents, told me that in so many words. My mother's youngest sister was only 5 months older than me. Yet, I was never one of them, and I felt a deep sense of loss of not having a sister too.

I didn't belong anywhere.

So, I tried my best to be accepted and would do anything for that. I made mistakes that I thought God was punishing me for when something went wrong in my adult-life. And loads did. This became a pattern of control. Trying to control everything meant I was safe. I was terrified of God, the Angry Man in the Sky, and did my best to stay under His radar.

I thought I was flawed, damaged and that I was not worthy of the good in life. Comparing myself with the school friends I wanted to hang out with, I became acutely aware of the huge difference in our parents, life-style, and money. I was less than. Once again, I did not belong. I was not accepted. I was forced to be friends with kids whose behaviour went against who I knew I was, but I had to belong somewhere and behave alike.

The church further shaped my self-image of not being good enough. Condemning any wrong-doing and condemning wanting money, which I knew would level the playing field, put me in a Catch-22. On the one hand I wanted to be rich so I could create a life that I desired, and on the other, I sabotaged my efforts because I believed I didn't deserve it and it would be wrong, and God would punish me. With all my mistakes I didn't want to stand out at all.

Yet, deep inside I had a knowing, a longing that this can't be it. That this is not what life is supposed to be. That I chose to live a life of fear and scarcity.

However, this was exactly the life that I created, until I was guided to another way.

My journey began when we lost everything after a business-transaction-gone-bad. I came from a lucrative career as an IT professional. My husband built a hugely successful IT consulting company. We were quite affluent. Life was good. Then disaster struck, and we were reduced to scarcity and fear.

Looking for answers about who we are and how we create our lives, my husband and I studied Neuro-Linguistic Programming (NLP). I continued my research and studies into the mind, neuroscience, quantum physics, Psychoneuroimmunology (PNI), Universal Laws, Energy.

I didn't buy into the boxes I was put into by experts. I understood from studying PNI that because of the scarcity and fear I grew up with, I wanted to control everything. But I didn't believe that I would satisfy my needs at the cost of others. I couldn't believe David R. Hawkins's theory that people can't change their vibration permanently. That meant that my life was doomed to be small and filled with fear and scarcity.

Although this rollercoaster pattern of abundance and scarcity continued to run in our lives for many years, I realize now that it was for my spiritual learning to discover my soul essence, that my husband suffered his losses. Again and again some unfortunate event cut off his prosperity, and I would be plunged into fear, guilt, shame, and powerlessness.

I started working with a coach who was on the same quest as me: to crack the code of abundance. I uncovered that most of my beliefs about God, my life, and money were false and that I have created a False Self that was not in alignment with my Soul Essence and energy vibration.

I learned that my thinking patterns were conditioned to focus on lack and the absence of what I wanted. That I allowed current results to control my emotions. At the same time, I tried to control everything else. I didn't feel safe to trust God—He was mad at me, remember?

Letting go of anything external controlling my emotions that evoke fear and doubt is an ongoing journey and the daily practice of faith and BEING in the energy vibration frequency of my joy and abundance. I now love the Unknown as the Certainty of Infinite Possibilities.

I have found the Kingdom of God-in-me, and it's my happy place. Connecting to my heart and this incredible love that floods my body lets me know I am safe and loved.

I AM HOME AT LAST.

I know there is no limit to my expansion. This is the Universal Truth—we are limitless. We are unconditionally valuable. It's my passion to support coaches and experts to expand their businesses in harmony with their soul essence and pay it forward to their clients, uplifting humanity.

I create my HEAVEN ON EARTH, and so can you.

ABOUT THE AUTHOR

Dina is the founder of Soul Purpose Publishing and Coaching. She is the #1 Amazon International Bestselling Author of the multi-author book; My Mess is My Message.

Dina works with successful entrepreneurs to elevate their brand, visibility, income and impact by becoming a bestselling author. She publishes multi-author and solo books.

As a Certified Quantum Leap Transformation Coach, Dina specializes in Soul-Alignment for Business Success. With 2 decades of neuro-coaching experience and her own journey of healing the fear of unworthiness, she believes that this is the biggest obstacle to success. She created the 5 Steps to Manifest a New Reality as a process and system that she uses in her coaching programs.

Dina is passionate about expanding the consciousness of the world through her books and coaching.

Website: www.dinamarais.com
Podcast: www.apple.co/3JFw1bU
Facebook: www.facebook.com/groups/1860127917519690
Email: dina@dinamarais.com

8

MELISSA CHERNOW

DIVINE BY DESIGN: YOUR BODY TALKS

When a classmate died of cancer in middle school, I wanted **better answers.** Conversations were surface level and fleeting, especially as time passed. In the weeks and months following his death, it became clear grief was something people were barely comfortable acknowledging, let alone continuing to discuss.

But I still felt it in my body. The emotional pain, confusion, fear, and overwhelming sadness remained. I'd lie awake well past bedtime, ruminating in the "what ifs" and "whys". Forty-nine sheep, fifty sheep... I had more success wearing myself out with the mind chatter and unanswered questions than I did counting sheep. My skin felt alive, buzzing with an electric pulse from which I couldn't unplug. Tension and tingles, my relationship with anxiety was off and running. Besides my mom, I kept these experiences to myself. Nobody else was talking about their experiences with grief, so I took the hint and kept quiet. Yet I wondered, was anyone else struggling in silence? Was it impacting them in similar ways?

Fast forward six years to a late August soccer practice. I went up for a blind header, my vision obstructed by a defender going for the same ball. My impeccably timed jump proved to be perfectly heartbreaking.

I won the header but lost much of my highly anticipated senior year. I didn't feel right. No stranger to concussions, I instantly knew the gravity of the situation thanks to my three previous head injuries.

My brain fog blossomed in the following days. Consistent headaches and immense pressure convinced me my eyes and ears were on the verge of exploding. I searched for safe spaces to retreat from the hustle and bustle of high school that would still allow me to remain somewhat present with my classmates. I napped in the nurse's office if I wasn't going home early. I'd go to the bathroom in the middle of class just to walk in the quiet halls whose lights didn't hum as loudly as they did in history class. The slow-paced and silent library became a safe haven. Sunglasses became my favorite accessory, shielding me from bright lights that had an unnerving way of piercing through my eyes and crawling down my spine.

I was incredibly uncomfortable in my body, not to mention the situation at large.

～

And then there was the simple but seemingly weighted question everyone kept asking me. Part of the reason I value deep conversations is because of how many empty conversations followed, "How are you feeling?"

I knew the inquiry came from a place of genuine care, but five months after sustaining my fourth concussion and still unable to exercise or complete most school work, the frequency with which I heard that question was as dizzying as my head felt. My symptoms weren't changing and neither were my answers. The smile I falsely wore may have fooled some, but those close to me knew the truth behind my glossy, absent eyes.

Countless doctor's appointments left me hungry for answers beyond, "Hang in there. Let's see how you feel in 2 weeks." I was fed up. Once it became clear that time offered more healing than the medical system could, I knew something had to change. Ironically, I knew it started with my brain; my mental approach held a major key in shifting my experience.

I stopped resenting my circumstance despite feeling subject to it. That meant accepting it and recognizing the ways I was in the driver's seat. I allowed myself to grieve, fully feeling my anger, sadness, and frustration. I curiously and more intently listened to the quiet voice within that told me there was gold to be found here.

There were four people whose wisdom was soul food through it all: the friend who answered every tear-filled phone call and held me as I cried; the friend who indulged me in low key adventures, dousing my days in smiles and laughter; my mom who stayed close and steady through it all; and the teacher who asked if I'd considered delaying college by a year to give my body more spaciousness as I recovered. That was the first time it really clicked: what if I started compassionately listening to my body rather than trying to force its healing?

Listening, laughter, presence, and perspective.

Without these, it's easy to think life is happening to us rather than for us. My anchors and lighthouses, I leaned into the listeners, the laughter, those present, and those offering sage perspective. I started asking better questions, sharing honest answers, vocalizing my needs, and allowing myself to receive what *I* deemed as supportive (the big four mentioned above).

I laughed a little the next time someone asked me the infamous four word question. While I don't remember my exact response or how I was feeling that day, I do recall feeling liberated after being more truthful in my response. I began creating pockets of joy and recognizing the small wins within every day. My concussion opened the door to a more meaningful life.

～

Two years ago marked yet another opportunity to deepen my relationship with my body and voice.

Though unrelated, the symptoms that were surfacing were just as invisible as my concussion symptoms had been. They were even invisible on bloodwork, which consistently came back in conventional range. Doctors simply left me with a, "I hope you feel better. Come back if anything changes." I didn't like that answer, and I knew my symptoms weren't normal. My inner voice urged me to look elsewhere for solutions, so I started doing my own research and spoke with those vocal about similar health journeys.

It wasn't long before I found myself back in the doctor's office during another flare. Finalizing yet another script for bloodwork, my doctor inquired, "Is there anything else today?" There it was... the door asking me to bust it open. I took a deep breath before requesting three additional blood tests (ones I'd been curious about given my research.) Squeamish as could be, asking for more bloodwork in itself spoke volumes. But at some point your purpose and mission outshine your fear. It's not that the fear doesn't exist, but it's choosing to take action from the place of possibility and your greater vision rather than from fear.

Ten days later, two of the three labs I'd requested came back out of range. *My body knew all along. It just needed me to trust it and take action in alignment with its needs.* With those results, I've been able to address the root cause of my symptoms. Beyond having a medical professional finally validate my symptoms in a way that offered tangible and necessary solutions, this was far more about me listening to my inner voice and unapologetically advocating for myself in the pursuit of sustainable solutions. I am an expert in my body. As you are in yours. Forever a student, learning from its wisdom.

I now appreciate how this all unfolded in my favor. The sacred redesigns are divine by design, and they open the door to your most magnificent and meaningful life.

ABOUT THE AUTHOR

Melissa Chernow is a Voice + Visibility coach, author, and the founder of Cardinal Publishing House. She empowers leaders to speak from the heart with confidence and clarity. She creates impact-driven books that reveal the many textures of humanity while inspiring authors and readers alike to live more authentically, joyfully, and within their soul's integrity.

Website: *www.melissachernow.com*
Instagram: *www.instagram.com/melissamelrose_*

9

TERRIE SILVERMAN

FEAR & ADVERSITY: AN INVITATION FOR THE COURAGE TO LEAP

"I am not a courageous person by nature. I have simply discovered that, at certain key moments in this life, you must find courage in yourself, in order to move forward and live. It is like a muscle and it must be exercised, first a little, and then more and more. All the really exciting things possible during the course of a lifetime require a little more courage than we currently have. A deep breath and a leap." - John Patrick Shanley

I t was the perfect job, because I adore coffee. I get to sip it, smell it, and most importantly, *Barista* it. The word itself sounds like a celebration. Ciao Bella, I'm about to become a Barrristaaa!

I was expertly trained to make aromatic, glistening, mahogany-colored beans become cappuccinos, lattes, café au laits, macchiatos, espressos, americanos and iced mochas

And who did I get to make these gourmet java drinks for? Meg Ryan, Julia Louis-Dreyfus, Dennis Quaid, Olympia Dukakis, Ralph Nader, Mickey Rourke and Genevieve Bujold (her name is so fun to say) because the coffeehouse was in an affluent neighborhood and across the street from an elite pre-school.

I felt virtuous and hip. I believed I was a part of a social justice movement. This was the 90s, so it was important to sip your coffee at an independent establishment and not the Godzilla that was Starbucks, which would open a store within a block of a neighborhood coffeehouse and frequently, the local place couldn't compete and would go out of business.

I was exceptional. I worked on a $10,000 cappuccino machine, all brass and sparkly. I knew exactly what I was doing. And I was fast. I could make three drinks at a time. The customers *oohed* and *ahhhed*, dazzled by the velvety foamed cappuccinos I'd hand them.

The job was physical and required efficiency, patience and grace. I'd carry 10 pound bags of ice, lug gallon milk jugs. I'd grip, tamp and tightly twist the portafilter filled with espresso, hundreds of times a day. I'd keep the line keep moving with a smile, remembering the regulars' drink preferences, six days a week.

This work worked out, because it allowed me to pursue my art. I was constantly taking workshops and writing and performing stories about my life at a number of the grooviest performance spaces in L.A. I was on my way.

Except that every day at 5 p.m., when the coffeehouse closed, I'd start the process of cleaning. And no matter how well you cleaned the day before, you had to start all over again. The Coffeehouse was like the plant in Little Shop of Horrors, that keeps saying, "Feed me, feed me!" It was incessant and insatiable.

I would mop, scrub, wash, rinse, dry, polish and sweep, all the while, picturing myself fifty years in the future, wearing thick, white orthopedic shoes, still sweeping the coffeehouse floor.

This daily dystopian image made me feel trapped, full of dread and burned out. But then I'd think, How can I quit? I can't leave my boss in the lurch. She relies on me. I'd have to give her a few months notice. And what would I do next?

Barista-ing for the past five years, meant that I was 5 years behind in computer skills and the latest word processing program, so I worried about how hirable I was.

But the thing about me is that I don't quit. I'm so afraid of not being able to pay the rent, and support myself, that I push through the drudgery and discomfort. And of course, avoid change at all costs, for change is terrifying.

I was loyal, unhappy and horribly burned out, which caused me to be a bit surly, particularly to the customers who were oblivious to good manners and cleaning up after themselves and their children. My boss insisted that I smile more. Smile, no matter what.

You don't know how demanding people are, until you've had a service job.

I kept on, until one day I dropped a bowl. I must be clumsy. And then I dropped a coffee mug. I watched it shatter all over the floor. That's when I realized my hand was involuntarily releasing whatever I was holding.

The next day, my whole arm throbbed, but I went to work because I'm a ridiculously responsible employee, and by this point, the manager of the coffeehouse. My right hand began to hurt so much, that I needed two hands to do everything. So I called my doctor, who told me to go immediately to urgent care.

When I told my boss, she asked me to drop off the bank deposit on my way. She was a philanthropist, she went to church, she hired a homeless woman, so I thought she was benevolent.

It was the first time in five years that I said "No," to her. It was clear that I had to take care of myself, since her priority was her business.

I was unable to work and within two weeks of exclusively relying on it, my left hand went down as well.

When your body is injured, you discover all the miraculous things it does, that you'd taken for granted. You do not know how many muscles it takes to pull on socks or hold a spoon to feed yourself.

The injury made me anxious, depressed and caused insomnia. I couldn't stop worrying.

My doctor ordered tests to check for all the scary possibilities: Lupus, Multiple Sclerosis, Rheumatoid Arthritis. The day of my tests was the same day it was announced that Annette Funicello had Multiple Sclerosis, so I pictured Annette and I sitting in our wheelchairs, rolling down the hospital hallway together.

The test results showed that I didn't have any of the debilitating diseases. Hallelujah!

What I did have, was a repetitive motion injury, Tendonitis (similar to Carpal Tunnel Syndrome) as a result of the cumulative holding, gripping and twisting required of an excellent barista.

I had to wear braces on both hands. When strangers asked me about them, I'd say my injuries stemmed from conducting an orchestra. No one ever questioned this explanation.

While this amused me, it did not reduce my fear and terror. I was petrified. How am I going to support myself when my hands don't work? Going back to that job was out of the question, but I had no idea what I could or should do.

For months, I'd take long walks every day. I'd scan the sky, looking for clues, stare at the roses for salvation, listen to the birds for hope. I'd place my aching hands on the trees, hoping nature would give me an answer.

Friends would throw runes for me, do tarot readings, pull Native American Medicine Cards. I'd spend afternoons at a tea house decorated with Paddington teddy bears, sipping Darjeeling tea, hoping someplace, somewhere, someone, or even one of the teddy bears, could tell me how I was going to support myself.

I was a distraught detective, in search of signs, solace and guidance.

I took the Myers-Briggs test, which was painful, because I could barely hold a pencil, but I desperately wanted answers. I don't remember which of the MBT types I was: ISFP, INFP, ESFP—something with an I or an E, but it didn't give me a clear path. It just indicated I liked to learn.

So I thought, I know what I'd like to learn: sign language, so I could become a sign language interpreter, imagining myself doing those beautiful, expressive gestures. Until I found out it too can cause a repetitive motion injury.

So that led me to consider becoming a Speech Therapist—that sounds important. But when I researched the coursework and discovered all the science and anatomy classes required, I decided that was the end of that.

During my quest for a new career, I found out that my teacher Nancy Agabian, who I'd been studying with at Beyond Baroque Literary Arts Center, was moving to New York. She inspired me to write and perform about my life, after I'd seen her to write and perform about her life.

Nancy's class was a godsend to me. And the fact that Beyond Baroque would no longer be offering a writing and performance workshop, would be a huge loss to the community. This just won't do. So I contemplated a crazy idea. What if I took over for Nancy?

Teaching, however, was the only thing my mother told me never to do, because she'd been a burned-out Second Grade Teacher.

Every Sunday night, as I sat under the Jiffy-Pop shaped bonnet of the portable hair dryer, watching the Ed Sullivan show, a fog of depression filled the apartment, because my Mother, a single parent, dreaded returning to the overcrowded, chaotic classroom the next day.

A combination of desperation and wanting to help, motivated me to ask Nancy what she thought about me taking over for her. She knew I'd never taught a workshop before, so I have no idea why, but she thought it was a great idea.

I didn't tell Nancy that I thought I was far too selfish to sit there and listen to everybody else and then watch them go up onstage. Plus, I could barely pay attention during class. I was so focused on whether my writing was any good, that I didn't hear what anyone else was reading. And after I'd read, I'd replay in my head all the feedback I'd received from the class and Nancy, completely missing the next participant's work.

I did not know if I could teach, whether I'd be good at it, or even like it. And it's not like I ever wished, wanted or prayed to be a workshop facilitator, but I told myself that all I had to do was try.

The only thing I was absolutely sure of, was that my next job had to involve my brain, not my body.

So I took the leap.

I Carpe Diem-ed, by writing the executive director of Beyond Baroque about my interest to offer a workshop after Nancy left. When I didn't hear back, I wrote the most passionate, persuasive letter I could muster. I don't know if it was my letter, or Nancy's recommendation, but the executive director finally responded with a 'Yes.'

I sent him a list of workshop names, which included many bad ones like *Create To Support Your Urge*, *A High Rise Of Stories* and the very worst one: *Letting Art Out*, which I realized sounded like "*Oh, poor Art, he's trapped, we must let him out.*" We settled on the simplest one '*Life Stories.*'

I put flyers all over town. I asked every facilitator I'd studied with, for teaching tips and writing exercises.

On October 9, the day the executive director selected for my workshop to start (which I loved, since it was John Lennon's birthday) I enter the pitch black performance space, turn on the lights and arrange the chairs in a circle, just like Nancy did.

I look at the five women and two men looking at me. As I welcome them, I can feel the presence of all the great teachers I've had, rooting for me.

Most importantly, I can feel the presence of Dennis Clontz, my playrighting teacher, my Annie Sullivan at the water pump, who helped me get what was in my head onto the page, after a lifetime of feeling paralyzed, stupid and full of self-loathing every time I'd try to write. So I'd eat so many donuts I thought I would die and then feel far too nauseous to even attempt to write.

Dennis took me under his wings and changed my life. He guided, nurtured and championed me to become what I thought was impossible. A writer. And thank goodness, I'm able to do it donut free!

As I lead the workshop participants, I am surprised to hear Dennis' slow, calm voice in my head. It guides my speech, rhythm and demeanor.

I say things I didn't know I'd learned from Dennis, things like personal mythos, Aristotle's poetics, and how the creative process works.

I see the participants write down what I'm saying. I cannot tell you how thrilling that is.

I takes notes as they read what they wrote. Thankfully, I'm able to listen and offer supportive, focused feedback.

I am struck by each person's unique voice and beauty. Once you hear someone's story, they'll never look the same to you, because they're no longer a stranger.

A few of the participants are teary-eyed, as they read their work, which makes what they are sharing more profound.

I tell them tears mean you're writing about something that matters, that you're writing from a place of truth and depth, that you're giving others the courage to dig deep and be vulnerable.

I don't recognize myself. I've never felt this intuitive, grounded and centered. Angst, anxiety and self-doubt vanish when I am teaching.

I didn't realize how much I'd synthesized from all the workshops I'd taken. That I understood a facilitator's job is to make everyone feel special, honored and heard.

As I put the chairs away, at the end of class, I feel a strong sensation. After a few moments, I'm able to identify it—this is the same sensation you have when you're in love.

And that was it. I didn't make any big decisions or pronouncements. I simply told myself, *I want more of this.*

That was twenty two years ago. And I'm still in love. It's the joy of my life to be invited into people's stories.

I had no idea that my leap, which came out of adversity, would be an invitation for a life-changing Grande Jeté. And that it would mark the birth of Creative Rites Workshops & Coaching.

Pain, discomfort, fear and adversity are catalysts for us to leap.

So when an opportunity presents itself, we're invited to take action: to change, to risk, to leap.

Fear is a great guide. If there's fear, it means you're not playing it safe. Be proud that you're challenging yourself. And consider that the amount of fear is in direct proportion to the gold that's on the other side of it.

I believe taking leaps are the way we manifest *Sacred Redesigns* in our lives.

Sacred change comes about through our leaps of faith.

Leaping, by its nature, is trusting the unknown. If we don't take those leaps, we'll never know what we're capable of.

Our willingness to trust, as we leap, is a gift we're giving ourselves.

When I came upon the John Patrick Shanley quote, I felt redeemed. I've always felt shame about my fear. But fear and courage are intrinsically connected.

As Shanley suggests, we leap even when we don't think we have the courage. The courage arrives after we take that first step, which then propels us to lift off.

And you don't have to figure it all out to take the first step. That first step is about giving yourself a chance, giving yourself the freedom and grace to just *try*, to just *give it a go*.

Once you take the leap, magic happens.

In my case, *Leaping* led to:

- Being given the title of Artist-in-Residence at Beyond Baroque.
- Being accepted into an MFA writing program and having the Worker's Comp retraining money applied to the program, which *normally never happens*.
- Getting to work with extraordinary people, a number of whom have become close friends.
- What I do for a living is soul-enriching and the opposite of work.

What petite steps or grand jetés have you taken?

Be proud of all the places you've landed.

Get excited about all the places you have yet to land.

Keep giving yourself a chance to leap.

When you take a leap, you get to tell that story.

Here's A Writing Exercise To Remind And Connect You To Your Courage And Fierceness:

WRITING GUIDANCE

The philosophy behind doing a spontaneous writing exercise is to express, discover and get out of your head. It may also spark an idea or story. And you get to practice releasing the inner critic.

When you respond to a writing prompt (or journaling or working on a 1st draft) don't edit or censor, just keep the pen or keyboard keystrokes going. Allow the thoughts to tumble out without judging them.

Don't worry about trying to write well, or organizing your thoughts, because that will take you out of your creative impulse.

You can't create and edit simultaneously, because then you're using both hemispheres of the brain, which means the analytical and the creative sides of the brain clash and stop the flow of the creative impulse.

Editing and structure are essential, but they must come *after you've created*, not while you're creating.

Let the writing be messy and spontaneous, enjoy and be surprised to see where it takes you.

TO PREPARE

Relaxing and slowing down allows you to listen within and connect to your muse and creative instincts.

- Close your eyes and take a few moments to breathe slowly and deeply.
- Breathe so that your stomach expands, then exhale slowly. Do this for at least a minute or two, allowing your mind and thoughts to slow down and to release tension.
- As you exhale, allow what wants and needs to be released from the day, the week, the month.
- Consider doing a slow neck roll, clockwise and then reverse. Then do a shoulder roll forward, then reverse.
- Stretch and breathe into any places in your body that feel tight.
- Finally, congratulate yourself for making time to express the most beautiful parts of you:

Your creativity, your imagination, your voice, your experiences, your struggles, your wisdom.

WRITING PROMPT

Think about a time you took a leap. It could be a tiny step or a big leap, but something that registers to you as a leap. Let this moment or memory unfold in your mind's eye.

If It Interests You, Here Are Some Questions To Consider:

- What made you leap? (What were the circumstances that precipitated the leap?)
- What scared you? (or what was at stake) by taking this leap?
- What are you the most proud of by taking this leap?
- What changed as a result of the leap?

Write about taking this leap and see where it takes you.

If you go off topic and into a tangent or memory, run with it and enjoy where leads you.

BONUS WRITING PROMPT

- Make a list of all the times you've leaped. Write about this list and what's revealed and/or what portrait emerges from all the leaps you've taken.

AFTER YOU'VE WRITTEN

Is there anything you discovered or that got clarified from writing about this leap?

Consider Sharing What You've Written With A Friend Or Trusted Colleague.

If possible, read it to them, because being witnessed, saying our words out loud, is an empowering act.

Tell Your Stories. It's the way we understand ourselves, each other and the world.

ABOUT THE AUTHOR

Terrie Silverman, MFA, is a writer/performer, director, story coach, creativity facilitator and founder of Creative Rites Workshops & Coaching. She's guided thousands of individuals, from all over the world, as well as Groups, Organizations, Businesses, Coaches and Thought Leaders, to craft extraordinary stories that inspire, captivate and deeply connect the story giver to their audience and clients. Terrie loves helping clients access their authentic voice, discover the gold of their stories, talks or keynote presentations, and release the inner-critic from the fears, perfectionism and self-doubts that can shut down the creative process. Terrie also facilitates in-person & online workshops with animals as catalysts for Creativity, including *Pet Lit – Meditate & Write With Our Animals and Write & Laugh with Goats.* Los Angeles Magazine dubbed Ms. Silverman a '*Goat Innovator.*' Terrie's clients have written acclaimed memoirs, been featured in national publications, as well as public radio storytelling shows such as *The Moth* and *This American Life.* Ms. Silverman also develops and has directed award-winning one-person shows. Terrie is the producer and host of the long-running storytelling show *Gorgeous Stories,* now online. It is the joy of Terrie's life to be invited into people's stories.

Website: www.creativerites.com
Facebook: www.facebook.com/terrie.silverman
and www.facebook.com/CreativeRites
Instagram: www.instagram.com/terriesilverman
LinkedIn: www.linkedin.com/in/terrie-silverman-20a75b9/
YouTube: www.youtube.com/c/TerrieSilverman

10

ANDREA BLINDT

I grew up believing I was powerless; that only well educated, wealthy people, or those with prestige had the power to make choices for themselves in life. I spent the majority of my life doing what I was told to do by my family and society in order to survive, unknowingly keeping this limiting belief alive.

I checked off all the boxes required to have a great life. I graduated at the top of my class in nursing school and worked my ass off for the only available position, working on the pediatric oncology floor of a top hospital. I got married and began working to start a family, allowing myself to ease into the belief that good things came to those who worked hard. Except good things didn't come.

I suffered two miscarriages and was faced with one of the hardest decisions I had to make in my life and career. I loved working in pediatric oncology; the bonds I made with my patients and their parents were deep, nourishing, and lifelong. I grew spiritually, working beside these resilient warriors who had been dealt some crappy hands suffering cancer, intense pain, the loss of their freedom, and their childhood outside of hospital walls. Yet these brave souls smiled and found things to celebrate daily. My soul was ignited, and I felt incredible purpose until I was forced to choose between having a baby and continuing to work as an oncology nurse.

With my feet raised in stirrups and a light blue cloth draped across my abdomen, I decided to quit the job I loved to give my body the best chance at successfully carrying a pregnancy. My fertility doctor had just completed my pelvic exam and reviewed the steps we would be taking in the weeks to come. I cried on the table as he reminded me that I was hanging toxic chemotherapy daily. Chemotherapy is a drug used to kill cancer, but it is not biased, meaning it kills good and bad cells. The baby I longed to create was a collection of cells that I was surrounding with a toxic environment. The two miscarriages I had suffered were proof that something needed to change. "Come work for me," he said, "There aren't toxic drugs here; just hormonal women, like you!" The doctor and I laughed at his words, and I cleared my throat as I asked if I could wear pants if I decided to work for him. The room filled with laughter, and it was decided. I would leave pediatric oncology and enter into the realm of fertility nursing. I was leaving what many people saw as a "hard place to work" and entering into what so many believed was a place "full of hope and answered prayers." It was that and so much more, but it would take me years of pain and healing to fully understand the gift of that journey.

A few short months later, I had become a "walking study" for all of my patients. I was someone they could relate to; I had been like them. I'd struggled with infertility, suffered multiple miscarriages, and had overcome the rollercoaster of failed fertility cycles. I was the success story that pushed them through their hardest days, offering hope and showing that dreams could become realities. I was pregnant with twins, and my hard work was finally paying off.

My faith in life perked up, and I started to believe that good things could really happen. I ended up loving my job as a fertility nurse and developed incredible relationships with the couples I worked with. I worked alongside a world-renowned fertility expert and soaked in all of his knowledge, becoming his right-hand woman. I met patients with him and created custom protocols that were cutting edge and full of hope. I had become his "Hail Mary girl" and together we took on patients that no other doctor would treat. I believed for them, and our outcomes blew us all away! We were a dream team until everything suddenly came crashing down around me, and I was left scrambling to catch all the pieces.

I spent two months in the hospital battling preterm labor and advocating for my babies' lives while my medical team struggled to care for me. And then at 26 weeks, the doctor on call decided it was time to deliver them. I was alone and terrified. I begged for her to stop, to give me medication to slow my contractions, and to please call my doctor but she refused. Since I was at a Catholic hospital, a sister came into my room and prayed over me. I remember hysterically crying as I covered my head with the thin white hospital sheet wishing this was all a bad dream, and then being pulled back into reality as I felt my bed roll into the bright operating room.

Grace and Wyatt were taken from my warm body and placed into the neonatal intensive care unit, where they lived for five days. They were perfect in every way externally, but internally they were suffering. Multiple specialists came to give second opinions on their diagnoses and to offer their condolences regarding the quality of life they were experiencing. Listening to the grim prognosis each provider relayed, we decided to withdraw life support in order to end their pain. A few hours later, they took their final breaths, hand in hand, leaving me broken-hearted in bed beside their delicate bodies.

I wanted to die with them that warm September night, as the doctor and nurses came into the room and took their still-warm bodies down to the cold morgue. I escaped the hospital in a wheelchair, being slowly pushed through the bright warm lobby full of smiling expectant family members and friends who held balloons and signs until we reached the exit, and I was forced into the darkness; my grief threatening to swallow me. The ache I felt was too great, too limiting, too final. I didn't know how to live through the pain, but my body carried on unconsciously. My heart continued to beat, but it was broken. Air continued to fill my lungs, but they were deflated. Thoughts flooded my mind, but they were nonsensical. The world continued to spin, but for me, it had stopped.

At home, I experienced more pain than I had ever felt in my life. My mind fought to make sense of what had just happened while my abdomen throbbed; the sutures that held it together stretching and pulling as my skin healed. I walked into the bathroom and allowed my body to collapse onto the cold hard floor. Alone in the darkness, my craving for death had intensified and I allowed the pain of their loss to settle upon me, burying my broken body under the weight of my lost hopes and dreams. Eclipsed in that darkness, I pleaded for death to take me away. I sobbed for hours feeling the pain seep from my body through my eyes, while the incision in my abdomen etched a physical reminder of their existence deeper into my being. Immersing myself in the agony, I started searching for where I had failed, looking for what I had done wrong. I considered the reasons, the causes of such heartache. I didn't find the answers I was looking for; instead, I found roots that led me back to who I was created to be. Through eyes brimming with tears, I chose to see them. I didn't know how to honor them or what it looked like to nourish them but knowing they existed grounded me here to the earth in a way that forced my belonging in that moment. I inhaled, deciding to believe that I was worthy, that I had a purpose, and that through this pain, I would learn how to rise again.

Slowly I began making choices for myself that allowed me to honor my roots. I strengthened them by choosing nourishing thoughts, foods, and people to saturate myself with. In doing this daily, I started to experience new life. As I started to bloom, my ability to grow magnified and I realized I could only continue flourishing if I took the time to prune the areas of myself that were no longer serving me. By consciously trimming the unhealthy things in my life away, I was creating space for new growth to occur that was stronger and more vibrant than before. Today I garden my soul with intention and grace, enhancing the life I am creating. Through this cultivation, I am able to rise stronger, fuller, and more abundantly than I ever imagined possible.

My desire for you is that you would find your roots beneath any worldly darkness you might be experiencing. See them, honor them, and then make decisions that support them in growing deeper, stronger, and better than before. Saturate yourself in the things that bring life, and be willing to prune off any areas that are unhealthy and prohibit you from fully blooming. You are worthy. You are capable, and no darkness is too final that it cannot birth new life one day.

ABOUT THE AUTHOR

Andrea Blindt is a registered nurse, holistic health practitioner, best-selling author, and life and mindset coach, who empowers others through her own personal healing journey. Andrea supports patients as they discover ways to enhance healing in their lives by reclaiming their power; advocating for what is in their best interest, and learning the tools needed to be able to make decisions that are in alignment with their beliefs. This allows her patients to create abundance, experience tranquility, and live life with clear intention. Andrea is an international best-selling author, has been featured on Natural Health Radio, Conceive IVF, multiple podcasts and publications, and is a contributing author for a parenting magazine. She lives in sunny California with her husband and four beautiful children. She loves being in nature, reading, and inspiring others to live their best life today.

Website: *www.andreablindt.com*
Instagram: *www.instagram.com/andreablindt*
Email: *heal@andreablindt.com*

1 1

ANNE TEIJULA

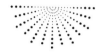

It is a dim old-fashioned pub with brown sofas and ashtrays all around. Melancholic Finnish countrylike songs play in the loud-speakers and billiard balls clatter. Speech and laughter fill the space. Snow and cold air enter the pub at the feet of incoming people. And that's where I cry, I moan, and try to tell confused explanations of my contra-dictory father and my dreams. I am on a first date, and I've become a little drunk.

My values are stolen from books and movies because my family has had such tight and strange values that I never could swallow. In my youth, we didn't have internet, and we barely talked about such difficult things with strangers. Even though we didn't have any books at home, I somehow managed to fall in love with books. I wanted to be as brave as Kwani in *She Who Remembers*, as wild as Pocahontas and wondering like Alice. I wanted to travel the world in 80 days and be smart as The Famous Five.

But let's go back to that pub... there was a long-haired man, Juha, who was confused but interested in me. We fell in love madly and deeply. He was loving and fun and bohemian. I got everything I needed. I got the liberty to be the real me; I got love, and I got jewels. And we talked, bonded, spent our entire time together, and we were really fond of each other.

I told him that I'd written a letter to my ex-boyfriend after our breakup. The letter was about everything I wanted to do instead of living in that small town and working for my parents. I still remember the feeling of being stuck in.

I wanted to write a book, to pet a koala; to see waterfalls, pyramids, and the jungle. It was more like my own bucket list. However, I never sent the letter; it wasn't meant to be sent. And there I was, now with a man who had similar dreams to mine.

We wanted to make some of our dreams come true. We tried to be wise and strong. We did everything we could to make things easy for my family and for their business—we made a plan where someone would stand in for me for work, and we could leave for almost a year to explore the world. But my father said no—absolutely not. No. No. Not even talking about it. My father didn't allow us many choices. It was always his way or no way at all.

Ok, we were gathering our thoughts again. I wanted to escape anyway. I quit my job in our family business and put my house on sale. The house was very important to me, but I sold it anyway. It was the cost of freedom. Freedom from my father, freedom of everything. But we got so much more life and experience for a change!

We moved to a tiny little cabin by the sea in the archipelago. Juha's father built it for summer holidays only, but we decided to live there.

Finland's summer is warm and bright, but the winter is harsh. We didn't have a bathroom or running water in the cabin, but we had each other. There we were, bathing on the snowy balcony at -20 degrees or in the sauna. We kept ourselves warm by sitting by the fireplace and drinking wine, laughing together and planning a trip around the world. We were happy.

But—there is always a but—I was diagnosed with cancer. I still wanted to travel as we had planned, but then Juha got a problem with his spinal code and had to undergo surgery. As if that wasn't enough, my mother started developing bad headaches, and it turned out to be a massive brain tumour. It was all too much to bear. I went back to my family's business to help out but my father kicked me out.

At that point, we decided to live as we had always wanted. My mother, Juha, and I survived our health issues, thanks to the great healthcare we received. Juha and I built our life on that island and travelled the world at the same time. We made that tiny cabin our home. We drilled a well and redesigned the cabin. I founded a firm and achieved my dream of writing books. We learned to read the weather and how to cope in the middle of nowhere—to be one with nature. We frequently traveled the world, from Asia to South America, from Africa to the Middle East. We drove through Europe to Spain to escape winter. We travelled to see wild animals and the beautiful starry nights in Africa, to experience spirituality in different religions, to smell the jungle, put our feet to the sand and hear the rhythm in the air. We travelled to Egypt to crawl into pyramids and snorkeled with dolphins.

To taste, to experience, to hear the world's voices. To try things new things. To search for the truth—where the boundaries are. To learn about the different people in the far reaches of the world. To find out what is big and what is important.

After more than a decade, our desires changed. It happened in Spain, during a stormy weekend. We got an offer for an apartment in mainland Finland, and we thought "hell yeah, why not?"

And we moved into an apartment in the city of Turku. We kept travelling around Europe, to meaningful places like Chernobyl and Auschwitz. Now, we have time for our hobbies, too—Juha loves old American cars, and I'm obsessed with theater.

What have we learned so far? Sometimes, the biggest obstacles drive you to the best adventures. Life should be mostly *hell yes* or *fuck no*, not just ok. Reach for the stars, and keep your eyes open. Dream and fulfil your wildest dreams even when nobody understands you. And when you sprinkle love and stardust into what you do, the world appears as a generous and magical place!

ABOUT THE AUTHOR

Anne Teijula is a solopreneur, author, and founder of Kevytkirjailija (which means "light-author" in Finnish).

She moved to a small island to the end of two ferries for more than a decade and learned to be free, idle and herself. Nowadays she is back in the mainland of Finland, enjoying city-life with culture and art and empowering entrepreneurs and freelancers. Anne remained lessor for an inn and lifestyle shop in Korpo island.

She has written a tarot-like book *Oomph Oracle*, a book of Korpo island, and self-help books. Her next mission is to gather amazing people to tell their stories and make miracles with books.

Anne's heart beats for theater, where she is also an amateur actress. Some of the roles she has played are Male Professor in Cthulhu (Love-craft) and Auntie in Little woman (Alcott). Adventures, nature and animals always get her attention and love!

> **Website:** *www.teijula.fi*
> **Email:** *anne@teijula.fi*
> **Twitter:** *www.twitter.com/AnneTeijula*
> **Photo:** *KasvotKadussa©JaskaPoikonen*

1 2

CAMBERLY GILMARTIN

From an early age, I have felt the presence of forces much greater than myself and deeply connected with them. I feel these vibrational forces especially high while in nature, in forests, at the tops of high mountains, and near water of any kind. I have physically seen and walked with Angels. And I can tell you that the energy of these beings is certainly something to behold and feel. When with these forces, a flow of information, questions and answers continually spring forth. I have learned to intuitively trust the information they provide.

Along the way, I've come to understand, at a conscious level, that what I have experienced is a connection with my heart space: soul, power, divine essence, spirit. I invite you to replace these terms with whatever you use to refer to this concept. It also became clear to to me that when connected to my heart space, all at once, I became deeply connected to every single atom, every human, plant, animal, and inanimate object on Earth and the sun, moon, and all the stars, planets, and galaxies in existence, and that the power of this unified connection provides answers, aid, and exists to serve humanity on a sacred level… and above all, offer abundance on every level. These forces are here to collaborate with us to shift and redesign our way of living so that we may create Heaven here on Earth.

To illustrate my experience with these forces and how they work alongside us when we are connected and open to their assistance, I share the following encounter with my Guardian Angel I had as a young college student.

A few weeks after my arrival in San Francisco, a new city to me, where I would attend college for the next three years, I accepted an invitation to spend the weekend with a high school friend who lived across the bay at UC Berkeley. On my way home from this weekend stay and unfamiliar with the transit system, I mistakenly got off the train too early and found myself in an unfamiliar part of the city. All around me, shops were boarded up, streetlights were dim, a smell of urine filled the air, and a crowd of street people roamed the darkened sidewalks. The street itself was extra wide, with four traffic lanes in either direction as well as two trolley track lanes in the center. I noted that there were no alleyways. The closed shops lining each side each had a metal gate and bars pulled down and locked over them. It was Sunday evening, so the city buses and trolleys were not running on their regular schedule. Oddly, there were no cabs, and little car or foot traffic to speak of. Besides the scattered groups of street people with heaping shopping carts, the street was eerily quiet. The only business open was a Burger King with a long line of people waiting to order. I got into line, figuring I'd ask the workers where the nearest open bus stop was. A minute later, I heard a woman scream, "I've been stabbed!" and a bloody hand was shoved directly in front of my face!

At that point, I figured that since I knew the general direction I needed to walk to catch the bus to take me to my college dorm, it would be wise to simply get going! Panic began to rise as I realized I would have to walk the five, extra-long, dark, city blocks alone. I could hardly breathe as I began walking quickly down the middle of the wide sidewalk to avoid sinister characters lurking in the shadows. Overcome with fears of never being seen again, I set out to walk the long blocks alone and began to pray, "God, please, please send your biggest Angels." I asked specifically for the help of Archangels Michael and Gabriel.

Halfway through the first block, suddenly as if out of nowhere, two men were at my side. The man on my left was Black and wore a white baseball cap, and the man on my right was White. Both were in shabby attire—and appeared a little 'rough' around the edges. They joined me, one on either side, pressing their shoulders into mine and perfectly matching my step. I was beside myself with fright and continued praying, asking for divine help. Not a word was said aloud by any of us for what felt like over five minutes. Then, while still walking, the Black man leaned forward and turned his face to look right into my eyes, and exclaimed "Hey, you're a freckle face! Us freckle faces gotta stick together."

It struck me as a very odd thing to say however in that instant, all fear evaporated as I realized beyond a doubt that I was safe and knew intuitively that I would not experience any harm whatsoever. An overwhelming sense of calm like none I had felt before took over. I could see the bright lights of a bus stop where an older woman was waiting for the bus that I needed to take to get to my dorm.

As we approached the lit bus stop, the two men fell back a step or two as I continued forward. I immediately turned to thank them, yet they were nowhere to be seen! This seemed mysterious as I had noticed én route that there were no alleyways, so they couldn't have ducked into one. The street was so wide that if they had chosen to cross it, surely I would have seen them doing so. And no cars, buses or taxis had passed us while we walked. The street had remained strangely silent. The men had simply disappeared into thin air. I felt like I had just experienced a 'twilight zone' episode.

This event remained a mystery to me until a couple of years later when in a bookstore I came across a book of letters people had written about Guardian Angels appearing in times of need, and I suddenly realized the identity of my two saviors. To this day I am fascinated that they appeared in shabby attire, and that the Black Angel had compared his freckles to mine to establish his identity. I realized that the Black man with the white baseball cap was Michael, my Guardian Angel. This was not my first, nor would it be my last, experience with Angels here on earth. However, it would certainly prove to be one of the most direct.

As I have continued to work to intentionally connect with these forces and live from my heart space, I've begun to notice that an inner "knowingness" informs me about every person and project I involve myself in or agree to work on. Within the last two years, it's become crystal clear that all things I am working on are connected. That we are all one. And that abundance exists everywhere.

It has also become apparent that those of us who are meant to work together are being brought together because the time to create a new world from our hearts is now! On that subject, it was four years ago that after a divorce, I ended up taking a new job where I met Nancy. The first day we met, we talked for two hours and intuitively realized we were destined to create together. This knowingness manifested into working alongside her and her business partner, Maybin. Their project, The Bellevue Urban Garden (tBUG), is a global community garden with a shared dream of universal importance: that the food we eat is inseparable from the land and conditions   it is grown in. And that healthy food is literally the root of healthy kids, families, community, wellness, and unity. This shared vision is much larger than it appears in mere words. tBUG is a place where people of all ages, and especially children and families, connect to their hearts, to the earth and to one another.

Maybin's story is one that deserves its own book. Since it is his story to tell, let it suffice to say that he used his heart, and connected to All, to get him from his homeland of Zambia to the United States. This voyage was necessary to fulfill a dream that began growing within him when he experienced a time of severe food insecurity. He truly understands how it feels to be hungry and see people suffer. He made a promise to himself that he would learn everything there was to know about growing food, and teach people how to grow healthy food. This became his life's goal. If you are lucky enough to meet Maybin, you will find his broad smile, twinkling eyes and energy contagious. The immense love he has for humanity and the planet is immediately apparent, and it's easy to be swept up into his dream for an abundant world filled with enough healthy food for all. His green thumb is more like a rainbow thumb and whatever he plants takes the shape of a colorful masterpiece. He has a child's joyful heart and zest for life.

Maybin and Nancy met at the Northwest Flower and Garden Show. And like my first meeting with Nancy, she and Maybin also realized in that instant that they were working on the very same dream and partnered immediately on the development of an educational program based on kale seeds to teach children, youth, and teens about growing healthy food and the concept of unity and abundance. Experiential education around growing food and the concept of it being grown in beauty ultimately has become a trademark of the garden known as tBUG. Nancy is an artist and illustrator and the best description of her is that of a beautiful, real-life grown-up fairy. Her sparkling eyes and heart shine brightly, and she possesses creativity, wisdom, and a consistent calm. These two people have taught me so much about building a dream, abundance, plants, beauty, health, unity, and connection over the last four years.

Nature, the human body, health, and the mystery of all living things have always fascinated me. As a child, I was either outdoors, playing with animals, creating something, or reading. At the age of 12, I read *The Chinese Manual of Medicine* cover to cover, memorizing every herb and plant and how they could heal the body. Healthy foods and keeping the body healthy has always been of utmost importance. So, meeting Nancy, and shortly after Maybin, and joining in to grow tBUG was a natural fit.

As a culture, we have grown disconnected to the foods we eat and as a result, many of us are not nourishing our bodies at a deep level. As we have begun to rely on technology, we have moved farther and farther away from growing our own foods, resulting in the ingestion of more processed foods, which hold less overall nutrition. We are vibrational beings and since all things also hold vibrational energy, we receive superior nutrition when we eat fresh fruits and vegetables that have been grown in clean soil without pesticides. Years and years of research on the use of chemicals and pesticides has been conducted, and yet there is little change on the planet. Cancers, reproductive issues, multitudes of insect and animal species becoming extinct, our oceans on the way to their death, and yet there seems no end in sight to our nonstop production and consumption of chemicals. The last few years of the global pandemic have allowed for a brief pause. Without humans by the droves, some places on the planet saw a return of nature—wildlife, a rejuvenation of sorts, at least at a small level.

The human body is an amazing thing. Our natural immune system, with the help of regular, healthy nutrition can rejuvenate itself in the same way nature does. Though I do not profess in any way to be an expert on the topic, I have spent my life learning and caring for my body and the bodies of those I love at a deep level and have experienced the power of a healthy immune system. The body is capable of rejuvenation when given the proper nourishment it needs.

My heart's desire is to inspire others to connect with their hearts, create a life of health, joy, and peace, and raise the vibration of the planet. Healthy nutrition is of crucial importance since a healthy body works in tandem with a healthy mind and these two things make it much easier to connect to our heart. When we connect with our heart, we raise our own vibration, we connect with all—in turn raising the vibration of the planet. If enough of us practice self-care at the level where we can live connected to ourselves and one another, we can create heaven right here on earth! tBUG is a mini version of this vision.

Close your eyes and imagine the future, the future of our children, grandchildren, and even their children. Imagine a world where everyone knows how to grow something. To grow something is to love and care for something outside of ourselves. It takes patience, hope, consistent care, and nurturing. When a seed that you plant sprouts, do you not feel proud and protective? What we grow, we love and nurture. We protect what we love. We must love the earth in order to be passionate about protecting it.

I recently had the experience of snorkeling amidst a pod of over a hundred wild spinner dolphins. Three days later, I had the chance to swim with a dolphin who had been born in captivity at Dolphin Quest, Honolulu. Experiencing these two events so close to one another was incredible and offered valuable insight.

Tears ran down the inside of my snorkel mask while amidst the wild dolphins. I had the thought that if everyone could see and experience the pure joy and love that emanate from wild creatures, we would each do everything in our power to protect them, to protect their ecosystem, the ocean—that mysterious beautiful body of water from which all life springs. Would we think differently about our use of plastic, our choice of foods, packaging, the products we purchase, if every one of us experienced this connection? I believe the answer is yes. The first part to making anything happen is believing it is possible.

In the world of the future, Heaven here on earth—that which we are already beginning to create today—we will live in a conscious way that allows for all other inhabitants of the planet to also survive and thrive. The thing is, though, we cannot continue going forward thinking, "I'm just one person; I can't make a difference." We all must come together and begin making different choices, knowing that we are going to have to give up convenience, but that by doing so, we are creating the opportunity to ensure our own health and the health of the planet going forward. We are currently the problem, yes. Yet we are also the solution, each one of us. It will take all of us. If we teach our children how to care for their bodies and minds at a deep level, teach them how to grow, harvest and eat healthy nutritious food and in turn how to reconnect to nature and to one another, they will develop awareness, empathy, love, true leadership, confidence, and a strong sense of self love. Where there is love... violence and hatred cannot thrive. When we learn to connect to our own heart, we can connect to the All, and the strength and the power of the unified forces is infinite abundance, peace, joy, and love.

tBUG is a visible slice of what the future can be when together we choose this way forward. Miracles are happening there daily. Teens are connecting to the earth, to life, to one another and most importantly to their hearts—discovering their true selves and understanding that they are enough just as they are. Families are connecting, people from diverse cultures are sharing recipes, knowledge, plants, and connection. Yes, plants are growing there, but so is love, and you can feel the love, beauty and abundance that is there.

I envision Maybin, standing in the garden smiling with a tiny seed in the middle of his outstretched palm talking to a group of young people. He is asking in a singsong voice, "Do you know what is inside of this tiny seed?" When the silence of the group settles without an answer, he laughs aloud and shouts, "LIFE! There is LIFE in that seed. And it is also in YOU!" Such a simple truth. Just as tBUG believes that the food we eat is inseparable from the ground in which it is grown, we too are inseparable from the foods we eat and the earth which provides for us. We are in fact, inseparable from one another, though we have been long taught otherwise. And we are inseparable from the forces that are here to assist us. When we connect to our heart... Joy, Beauty, Happiness, Love and Abundance is our natural state of being—it is who we truly are.

ABOUT THE AUTHOR

Camberly Gilmartin is an entrepreneur, business woman, parent, author, and active change advocate for businesses, people, and the planet. She has learned that action is what creates change and believes that the world is ready for a shift at a big level. Her mission is to inspire others to connect with their hearts, create a life of health, joy, and abundance, and raise their vibration so that they may inspire others in their lives to do the same. If you would like to connect with Camberly to learn more, or collaborate on an upcoming project or business, you can contact her at the links below:

Email: camberly.gilmartin@gmail.com
Website: www.wgwbook.com/Camberly-gilmartin

13

CAMILLA FELLAS ARNOLD

I felt like I'd been fighting against the tide for years. I was tired of the struggle of never knowing who I really was or what I was meant to do with my life.

The only thing I truly knew was that by now, after a decade of freelancing, no employer would have me. I had become 'unemployable.' Luckily, working 9-5 for someone else wasn't my dream and was never going to suit the lifestyle I craved.

Equally, I knew that my self-employed career was going nowhere fast. I'd returned to freelance design work reluctantly after winding up my blossoming wedding photography business due to being plagued by anxiety and panic attacks.

There'd been no obvious reason for the panic attacks other than what I felt was the universe shifting me back to my soul's purpose—even though I had no idea what that was. My only skills were within the creative realms, but after so many years of struggling to make it work, my relationship with creativity was bordering more on hate than love. I had stopped creating for myself and for fun. The joy was gone.

A chance conversation with a client led me to what I thought was the answer when they asked me if I could help them design and publish their book. This didn't feel like a stretch as I'd spent many years as a freelance book designer, so I jumped in wholeheartedly and started building my vision for my own publishing house.

Things were steadily building, and it finally felt that I'd found my place in the world. Then the pandemic hit, and everything began to change.

My business had always focused on the production and publishing side of books, but in May 2020, I ran my first ever writing challenge. The idea had been born out of my father pondering how he could occupy his time while in lockdown and he'd mentioned revisiting a book he'd started many years prior but never got round to finishing. So for a month, I ran a challenge working with thirty-five people to help them write their books. It was an incredible experience!

After the challenge, I continued working with some participants in a mentoring capacity as they were still writing. But quickly, I found myself out of my depth due to my own limited writing experience.

Writing had been a lifelong dream I'd been cut off from as a child after a careless comment from a relative so I'd spent over twenty years trying to stay within the orbit of stories by designing the books that contained them. I'd always known in my heart one day this block would come back around and finally, here it was rearing its ugly head.

But I wasn't quite ready to face it so I decided if I couldn't *mentor* writers, I would *coach* them instead. I took up a coaching qualification to give myself a solid foundation to add writing coaching to my author services.

However, training to be a coach unravelled me more than anything else. The limitations and constraints imposed by the process encouraged my creative thinking to come up with innovative solutions to translate creative exercises onto the screen.

I began to see how everything I'd done and learned up to that point was culminating into this moment. I lit up at seeing my clients unlock their passions, embrace their creativity, and heal their inner child. Through all of this, with every client I helped, I began to heal my own wounds and unlock a new level of creative flow in myself.

And then I became angry. I looked at the journey I'd been on and saw the same struggles in my clients. So much of the creative industry seemed to function only to serve the end-user, rather than the creator.

I was angry at how my relative's offhand remark had stopped my writing dream in its tracks for more than twenty years. I was angry at how fragile these artistic dreams were and how easily someone else could decide a person's fate.

I was angry at how freelancers were so apologetic as they lowered their rates to peanuts to win work. I was angry at how little people valued creativity. I was angry at my own fear and inertia to face it.

It was then I realised it was time for me to face my fear and to make a stand. I remember walking in the afternoon sun, declaring to my best friend on the phone that I was a creativity coach and an advocate for the creative industries. I had no idea what to do next, but the inner peace I felt at saying those words meant I trusted I was on the right path.

Almost overnight, I walked away from seventeen clients whose books I had been producing and publishing, and I set about going deeply inwards. From the ashes of my publishing house rose the most creative period of my life thus far, creating a series of coaching programmes designed to help people unlock their creativity and ignite the spark within themselves.

As I did so, I found my own voice and began the *Creative Power* podcast to share my message far and wide. I wanted everyone to know they had creative potential within themselves and learn to unlock it. I wanted everyone to savour, celebrate and nurture creativity in a way the world has never seen. I wanted to activate my listeners to revolutionise creativity and the creative industries.

Moving forward with this message, my inner child has been liberated and my own creative practice has been galvanised. The joy of creating returned to me as I began to write poetry daily and mapped out a series of books to support creatives. It has felt like a long, winding journey and often didn't make sense but in facing my fears and claiming who I truly am in the world, I've finally found my soul's purpose.

ABOUT THE AUTHOR

Camilla Fellas Arnold, creative coach and podcast host for Creative Power. Using multi-disciplinary creative skills and coaching programmes, Unravelled Soul Journey and 90 Day Moon Writing Flow, she helps people unlock their gifts and achieve their creative potential. She holds BA (Hons) Design for Publishing, MA Communication Design and is an ILM Level 7 Executive Coach and Mentor.

She has over a decade of experience in the creative industries as a freelance graphic/book designer, professional wedding photographer, and publishing company founder. A passionate advocate for creative industries, she is a member of the International Society of Typographic Designers, Fellow of the Royal Society of the Arts and uses her unique expertise to support others embrace creativity in their lives.

Living in rural Norfolk, UK, with her husband and two Shetland sheepdogs, Camilla is embracing her life-long dream of being a writer/poet and sharing her voice with the world.

Website: www.camillafellasarnold.com
Email: hello@camillafellasarnold.com
Podcast: www.geni.us/creativepower
LinkedIn: www.linkedin.com/in/camillafellasarnold

14

CHARLI FELS

THE MODERN WOMAN REJECTS, RECONNECTS AND REDESIGNS

She's magnetic. She owns her strut.
She stands with an aura of confidence and knowing.
I am declaring right here that I am a Modern Woman.

Most of us are living in a vacuum, the vacuum of conditioning. You know that feeling when something restricts your thought, message, belief, and you can't voice it. The throat feels tight as if a boa constrictor has settled around your neck; you struggle with it, but it's got a hold on you no matter what happens. The vacuum of conditioning slowly consumes you. It slowly caresses your body and your mind and eventually consumes and drains your soul. There's an eerie sense of emptiness. It begins to expand, the air smells stale, the people look stale, the experiences feel stale, the opportunities are stale, the vortex of this vacuum is suffocation. For most of us, this is 'The Norm.' This vacuum controls emotions, minds, bodies and souls. It creates people pleasers, boundary voids, judgemental hearts, searing expectations and a monopoly of fear-based states of existence. This world has a sense of dystopia.

Let's face it: we're tired of congratulating the woman working in a male-dominated industry, striving for equal pay, equal opportunities.

We're tired of the condescending tones from our male counterparts who say 'well done' for jobs that we do matching what they do. I'm tired of the woman's income being seen as a subsidiary to the family budget. I'm tired of words of pity thrown at a woman because she's making intentional choices about her life, her finances, her career, her identity, her gender. I'm tired of listening to labels where the woman is seen as a Superwoman because we visibly see her multi-tasking, juggling the home, housework and career spaces. Labels like Boss Babe, Mompreneur or Business Bitch drinking wine, are spoken and announced with pride. These types of labels revolt me. Don't get me started on the topic of sexualisation of women. I was one of those young girls that had boxes of Barbie dolls and numerous outfits. I spent endless hours changing outfits and playing with the girls. Children play as a way of making sense of their world. I remember gently caressing Barbie's breasts, waist and hips as a young child, being fixated on her curvature. Of course, one day, when I grow up, I will look like Barbie. Ironically, I still have all my Barbie dolls and hand-knitted and handmade clothes made by my mother. I'm not sure why I still have them. Is it to remind me of this systemic conditioning I was exposed to or perhaps how much I have healed to grow?

This vacuum created a life filled with rejections. It recreated a lifetime of receiving the word 'no.' The spoken no, written no, the feel of no, over and over again. No, from bosses, colleagues, stakeholders, husband, daughters; I noticed I would simple redirect my energy and refocus on adapting, modifying or creating something else. Mostly to please others. I remember when I was 10 and I asked my mother if she would take me to the local library. She said 'no.' I contemplated this for a little while and then decided to walk myself. One kilometre and overbridge later. Or when a school principal said no to allowing our small students to climb trees. A serious injury could occur, and 'we don't want that on my watch.' I negotiated and asked that if I placed safety mats under the tree trunks and had an adult standing beside the trunk, we could still explore risk taking, problem solving and muscle building, couldn't we?

When I wanted to go to university after secondary school and my mother said, 'No, we won't be able to afford it', I actually was triggering her fears around education. University studies were fee free in Australia back in 1980s. I went to university and graduated with a Bachelor of Teaching Early Childhood. I went back to university at the age of 40 and obtained a Diploma of Visual Communication, then a Masters in Digital Design and Animation, then became one of Microsoft's Innovative Educators Experts in Australia. I don't settle for no.

Every rejection leaves a clue. We can be open to seeing it or be ignorant and blind. After 6 years throwing cutting edge technology proposals to executives at an elite private Boys' Secondary Education College, receiving rejection after rejection, I would ask myself why the rejection? Does the system need to change? Is the idea not worthy? Don't I have the skills? Is this impossible to execute? Could I have handle this differently? What's wrong here? What's wrong with me?

I don't fit into any box. Maybe that's why I had rejection after rejection. Being able to see clearly and have a perspective that each 'no' response I took was an opportunity to be redirected. I smile now in reflection, for the divine was gently nudging and redirecting me towards my soul's path and purpose. I couldn't see it. I was determined to create amazing things for this school. It felt like nobody was listening. I became more masculine-like to fit into the 'club.' I took professional development workshops to better understand the teaching of male students and working with male colleagues. Unfortunately, those who were teaching female educators how to respond to male students were males themselves and were coming from a male to male perspective. A punch on the arm as a kind gesture to a male student isn't a strategy that a female teacher would use towards a 15-year-old male student. I learnt how men congregated and communicated. I felt very comfortable interacting with men. Over the 6 years, my energy went from a balanced feminine and masculine energy state to functioning 95% masculine energy. I still got rejected.

THE MODERN WOMAN TAKES REJECTION AND TURNS IT INTO A REDIRECTION

Heart opened; I recall the number of times the divine sent experiences of rejection my way. The word 'no' has such polarity. I loathed it because it has controlling intentions but on the other hand, it's so juicy to claim the 'no.'

The fall of rejection led to redirection. I realised that I was relying on my external world to control my every move. Decades of rejection and emotional accumulation scored a deflated soul. It ended like an explosion. To reject the rejection was a powerful moment in time. It was the last day of being an employee.

My husband said to me, 'Are you going back?' I looked at him straight in the eye. My mind was still. I had no thought, no guilt, no self-judgement or fear. My body was trembling. I shook my head and said so calmly 'No.' I stood there and at that moment I was rejecting the employer. This rejection was my redirection. Yes, I am disrupting the course of the path I was on but ultimately it was a conscious decision that my rejection was my own soul's redirection. Tears were streaming down my cheeks. A sensation riddled my body. I knew this was a pivotal moment in my life. That evening we celebrated with champagne. We celebrated the future of the unknown. We celebrated the surrender.

My parents said no to art school when I was 17. I found myself an art mentor at 35 years old and studied with her for 2 years. I am an artist.

I received a bashing of rejectable 'no' to projects during my employment in the education sector. I started my own design business and built visual personal brands for people.

My manuscript and book ideas were rejected by publishing houses three times over a decade. I redirected and started my own publishing company.

FLIP THE REJECTION.

What if you flipped rejection on its head? Rather than being rejected, BE the rejector. Reject the norms, reject conformity, reject anything that doesn't serve you, your creation, your journey, your soul's purpose.

Looking back over the years, the word 'NO' was the catalyst for:

Wearing white vinyl boots at 5 years of age in a school running race
Learning piano at the age of 36
Applying to design school at the age of 40
Writing my first book
Producing book collaborations with 5-year-olds
Walking the alps in Switzerland
Starting my first business making and selling knitted tea cosies
Discovering I was a poet
Becoming an international best-selling author
Bottle-feeding my first child
Innovative teaching practices
Writing another proposal
Studying animation rather than HTML
Self-belief
Grit
The Snow White in me to wake up
The Cinderella in me to sparkle beyond midnight
Stand up to the big bad Wolf of fear
The princess owning her truth
The Goldilocks in me to overcame limiting self-beliefs and to feel just right
Puffing and steaming and chanting 'I think I can...'
Discovering my soul's purpose through scientific hand analysis
Feeling fearless
New vision
Shedding the tears
Shredding conformity
Touching my inner icon
Learning to surrender and receive from source
Receiving love and loving self
Strutting my truth
Being unapologetic

Many of my colleagues painted me as a rebel. Oh, did they get this so wrong. A rebel is someone who intentional disrupts without respect to cause pain or hurt. I'm an empath. I feel the pain and sorrow. I was curious of this perception. What they saw was that I spoke up. I openly discussed their methodologies, philosophies, pedagogies, systematic approaches. I questioned the status quo visibly in meetings. I'm one of those people who question everything. Think of that irritating kid that keeps asking why and never shuts up. I question what's beyond the surface? Is this true? Is there an alternative? What's the best scenario? What's the consequence? Where is this taking us? What do we need to build on to this proposal to make it juicier, richer? I disrupt thinking.

I thank my soul every day for this gift of being curious.

THE MODERN WOMAN IS CURIOUS.

She feels and thinks. She is in touch with her emotions and thoughts.

As Brene Brown says: 'Choosing to be curious is choosing to be vulnerable because it requires us to surrender to uncertainty.'

Embracing uncertainty and not knowing is an act of courage.

THE MODERN WOMAN IS COURAGEOUS.

Questioning the status quo is surrendering to uncertainty. And with this vulnerability often comes fear. The Modern Woman is vulnerable. She may fear disruption, discomfort, judgement, being shut down, losing promotions and opportunities, being bullied; however, the Modern Woman rejects fear.

She takes this fear and turns it into *reconnection*.

I had the fortune to work in the education sector. I wore a mask every day. I used to think this was fantastic. I could hide myself behind the mask, never revealing the real me in the public arena. This eventually had an effect of soul derailment. I became so familiar at being somebody on a daily basis, that after nearly three decades when I stepped out of the education arena, and removed the mask, I felt vanilla. Arggh! I invested time, money and energy in shadow work, spiritual and soul work, personal development, speaking and brand coaches, going deep to unearth limiting beliefs, sabotage, imposter syndrome and more. The journey of connecting to self is life changing.

THE MODERN WOMAN CREATES.

She takes this redirection and reconnection and turns it into the path of *redesign*. Intuition and soul divine guidance led my creation of doing business differently. I want to be on fire with purpose every single day. I stand knowing that I am co-creating with my source. I don't seek validation from others to reject my creation. I am anchored and aligned.

We are pursuing meaning, our own meaning of life and through this it's our own experiences that make us who we are. We don't fit into a box; we are not meant to be followers. We are here to honour ourselves and show to the world exactly who we are. We have no judgements or expectations placed upon ourselves or by others. We nurture and nourish ourselves. Feel the vibration of authenticity, of being unapologetic.

I guess Joseph Campbell, the creator of the Hero's Journey, would have termed this journey of rejection as my 'call to adventure.' I actually see the journey for the Modern Woman as stepping from the ordinary world (the conditioning vacuum) into the extraordinary world of sacred redesign.

Each rejection was one step closer to realigning my soul. It's not about the ego mind changing who I am but rather my internal self reaffirming and refining who I am, where I'm going and what I want. Stepping over the threshold does bring challenges, but it sets you free each time, escaping from habitual behaviours and actually seeing the realities of reconnecting with spirit. This reconnection starts with a conversation with the soul; it's the process of surrendering, receiving, releasing old beliefs and what no longer serves you.

If only we seek our inner gifts to build and create our destiny first. The co-creation is our creation; anything that we dream or imagine can be possible.

"Once you believe in yourself and see your soul as divine and precious, you'll automatically be converted to a being who can create miracles." - Wayne Dyer

The Modern Woman has emerged.
She is courageous.
She stands tall.
She's a showstopper.
She's proud of who she is.
She owns her strut.
She commands attention unapologetically.
She is the Modern Woman who is connected to self and soul.
She builds a relationship with herself first.

The Modern Woman flips convention.
The Modern Woman flips stereotypes.
The Modern Woman dissolves judgements from others and especially herself.
The Modern Woman flips expectations.
The Modern Woman puts fear on its head. She leverages fear to heal.
The Modern Woman connects to her soul. No more seeking validation.

She chooses herself and honours her significance.
She sees rejection as redirection.
She rejects the status quo.
She ditches the fear of judgement, rejection, imposter, not being good enough, fear of failure.
She celebrates her wins and successes.

She is bold and courageous.
She speaks her truth
She plays big.

She's able to redirect, reconnect and redesign her vacuum that I call STRUTOPHERE; her space, her creation, her mind, her body, her soul...her power.

She's magnetic.
She owns her strut.
She stands with an aura of confidence and knowing.

So, my darling woman, I ask you this question: who is the Modern Woman in you?

ABOUT THE AUTHOR

Charli Fels is the founder of OSTRICH180 Publishing. She is an International Best-Selling Co-Author of *Innovation Secrets* and *Uncensored, Untamed, Unleashed;* a world leading Brand Strategist and Identity Designer, and artist. Charli is known as the Modern Publisher for the Modern Woman as she flips traditional thinking and publishing on its head. She helps the modern woman to WRITE her book, PUBLISH it and MARKET it.

Working with the most exciting Leaders, Charli applies a holistic approach to unlocking and unleashing the author within, empowering their strut and embodying their inner icon so they can share their soul's message, movement and mission with fearless visibility. She works with solo authors and on collaborative projects, offering Amazon best-selling multi-author book programs.

As a mother of two daughters, one with a hearing impairment, Charli is an advocate for inclusiveness and diversity. She loves creating; whether it's in the kitchen, drawing with charcoal sticks, sewing her own clothes, rearranging spaces or decorating her home. Charli has discovered her love for writing poetry.

Website: www.ostrich180.com
LinkedIn: www.linkedin.com/in/charlifelsbrandon
Email: info@ostrich180.com

15

EMILY TUCK

When I was first introduced to the concept of epigenetics in 2019 during a Kinesiology CPD workshop, I didn't realise my family's lives were going to change. The class was called "Transforming DNA Memories," pioneered by Sylvia Marina.

This workshop was a way of unlocking from the subconscious, the genetically inherited patterns of life, the attitudes, the behaviours, the beliefs, the limitations, and the possibilities that we inherited from our ancestors.

Through hearing the story of our ancestors and releasing the limiting strands of DNA from our lives and bodies, and by choosing the ones that we're empowering and we're filled with instead with the potential within our DNA and within our family heritage.

We could rewrite our genetic code, and it is this story that I want to share with you because it was truly a sacred redesigning of my life, and that of my family, both for the generations behind me and the generations yet to come.

Over the years that I have used epigenetics for myself and in my practice with my clients, I have seen the power of their ability to redesign the lives of my clients and those of their families.

As I began to hear the story of my ancestor and the choices that she had made,

I began to recognize my family and their choices being repeated down the generations.

I recognized the feelings of frustration or limitation or lack of choice about life. I realised that these were her feelings. The choices she had made that had been integrated into her experience, and the ripples of those choices were playing out in her descendants generations later.

As I use this tool over the years, I've redesigned several areas of my life and now continue to support my clients in redesigning theirs.

I began by transforming whether my sense of how I could live my life was for the external approval of others or whether I was choosing to follow my heart—a choice she had tried to make but was ultimately afraid to fulfil.

In her time and life, she had accepted her father's view as having more authority over her life than her own. In clearing this for me, for her, for us both, I gave up victimhood.

My own sense of internal authority began to deeply navigate my life.

In these sessions, she whispered in my ear and gave me advice from once upon a time to tell me what she did and why? If she had her time again, what did I need to choose instead?

Over a concentrated period of maybe 12 months, I came back to this genetic coordinate, and I came back to this particular ancestor, although not exclusively; there were others who wanted their part in reshaping my future.

I watched my own life transform as a result of this sacred redesign.

I became more authentic; I became more honest; I became braver. I redesigned my business. My relationship with money, my relationship with myself; I rebuilt my possibilities with lovers and reactivated in our DNA the possibility for sacred sexuality and the ability to love with all my heart.

I reconnected to a dormant undiscovery deeply nurturing creative practice. One that once upon a time my ancestor was truly gifted in—she was a poet, a writer, an artist, and now I had access to all of this too.

What I hadn't anticipated was how that would also ripple forward and backwards.

I predominantly dealt with my dad's DNA strand, and I found in discussions with my dad later that he was also feeling that he could be more honest, more authentic, and be open about his feelings.

He also felt less angry, less frustrated, less stuck with all sorts of things in his life.

He had begun independently, apparently, to percolate on what life meant to him, whether or not he had done a good job at being a father and whether or not he was like his own. He had also taken up art, which he hadn't done since school!

Over the months, I redesigned and reshaped my relationship to exercise to food, which my ancestor had used as a way to suppress her natural potential, as it was unwelcome in her home.

If I'm not allowed to be somebody that I choose, then my potential cannot come to the surface.

I found out using epigenetics that this use of food to hide my personality and my potential and my authentic self was activated in me at 8 years old, and I began to overeat too. I was living out her decision.

And as I worked on that particular strand, over a course of weeks, my father came back to me and reported that he had suddenly decided it was time to get fit and bought himself exercise equipment. He started eating healthily and promptly lost 4 stone in 6 months.

I don't have any children of my own, but a client recently shared with me that after we had been using epigenetics as I had told them to, they reported their mood, which had always been a little depressive by nature, was shifting. However, they had also been contacted by both their sons, seeking advice about how to improve their own low mood. Here was the ripple transforming him and a new choice going forwards into his children.

I have also had people work with me prior to conception as part of family planning to clear out limiting frameworks, or fears they carried so that they have neutralised them before their DNA is passed on to their children. Conscious parenting at its best!

It is a privilege to witness these sacred redesigns of family templates for generations past, present and future, to observe children give their parents a second chance to fulfil their potential, to witness parents choose again for a better future for their children. What redesign do you and your family and future generations desire?

ABOUT THE AUTHOR

Emily Tuck has been a holistic practitioner since 2004, having trained in multiple modalities. Understanding the true power of the subconscious, she transformed her life when she dedicated herself to focusing on being powerful, loving and manifesting a successful business, and she began to create her own reality. Emily now has a successful online business and practice, with several group programmes and limited spaces for private 1-one-1 coaching.

She also hosts a podcast called Lilith Speaks.

Emily's mission is to teach people to build a relationship with Lilith and show them how they can embrace their own inner power to transform their businesses, creativity, relationships and lives.

Emily is passionate about this beginning for people as early as possible and so also offers these holistic modalities and insights to families and teens.

Website: www.emilytuck.com
Podcast: www.geni.us/lilithspeaks
LinkTree: www.linktr.ee/thewomanemilytuck

16

EMMI MUTALE

EMBODYING MY SACRED FEMININE POWER

I lay in bed, utterly exhausted. I could feel my energetic fuel tank running on empty and sensed my life force, that sacred elixir that kept me alive, slowly ebbing out of my body.

Behind me was another 12-hour day at the office, another unfinished to-do list, another queue of unanswered emails, each claiming importance over the other.

Ahead of me, an endless evening of two small kids vying for my attention and a disgruntled husband who knew better than to try and engage me for anything but a brief chat about the following day's commitments.

I knew something had to give. In fact, I'd felt a strong urge to step out of the hamster wheel, to exit the unrelenting, unforgiving routine for a long time.

Yet, a part of me was addicted to the thrill of climbing the career ladder, receiving praise for my accomplishments, and having a fancy title that evoked a sense of importance.

That part of me was on a constant mission to find validation and meaning outside of myself.

That part of me truly believed that I did not matter and had done so from an early age.

You see, home wasn't always safe growing up...

With my Dad's undiagnosed mental health issues, tendency to drink when stressed and frequent bouts of violence, I learned to walk on eggshells and speak in a hushed tone since I was a little girl.

I also learned that Dad's military-like authority was not to be questioned, that the right to show anger was reserved to him and him alone, and that what the neighbors thought of us was always more important than me expressing my rage or my joy.

I became an expert in assessing the energy in a room before entering, knew how to keep my emotions to myself and was wise enough to teach my little brother to keep his mouth shut if Dad was in 'that mood.'

In this black and white world of rules and restrictions, power and authority belonged to men, the government always had our best interests at heart, the 6 o'clock news were the only reliable source of truth, and women were to be financially dependent on their husbands.

Unbeknownst to me at the time, I took on the belief that speaking my truth and expressing myself authentically was not safe, and that my wishes and needs were not important—and this belief formed the foundation of my life as I grew up.

Time and again, I silenced the voice that kept on whispering to me that I had a bigger purpose and that my intuition was my True North, even when it went against the grain and challenged long held notions around what it meant to live in this world. I continued to make myself small so that I would not rock the boat, challenge the narrative, or make myself unlikable.

In many ways, I still ended up doing exactly what I wanted: I excelled in school, obtained a Masters Degree from a prestigious University, built an international career in the field of human rights and moved to Africa, fulfilling a childhood dream. By the time I was 32, I had married a man I loved, had two beautiful children and a career that inspired me.

And yet, in my early 40's, I found myself in bed, with my life force tangibly ebbing out of me...

That was a turning point.

I knew that my way of living was not sustainable and that I was dishonoring my journey, my body, and my true calling at a deep level.

I was starting to understand that I had led my life from action- and results-oriented masculine energy, constantly pushing myself beyond my limits and ignoring my feminine essence that was yearning to be recognized.

I had not yet embodied the importance of *being* instead of *doing* nor connected with the sacred voice of my womb, but I *did* realize that I was doing a disservice not just to me but to all those I was truly meant to serve.

I decided to take a leap of faith, quit my job and start a full-time healing and transformation business that had been sprouting inside me for 10 years. I gave myself permission to follow my body's rhythms and shape my business accordingly. I chose to take action from a place of deep inner harmony and knowing, harnessed the power of all the healing modalities I had studied since my early 20s, and started listening to my womb in her infinite wisdom.

I healed those parts of me that were still wound up in a tight bundle of nerves, feeling unworthy and afraid to speak my truth, and chose to use my voice and presence for healing. And once I embraced my feminine essence, the path of true service—guiding women to connect with the sacred feminine wisdom inside their wombs, heal lifetimes and generations of wounds that stop them from loving themselves and to step into their sacred feminine power—opened up.

My womb, my sacred cauldron of feminine wisdom and power, is now my guiding light—she speaks to me, nudges me in the right direction and continues to remind me of who I truly am; an infinite spark of the Divine whose body is sacred and sovereign.

Try this:

WOMB LISTENING

Place your hands over your womb and close your eyes. Take a few deep breaths, allowing your body to relax. Tune into your womb space, feeling her energies. Breathe in and out of your womb a few times and say hello to your womb, smile at her. And then just listen. What is she telling you?

You may need to give your womb some time to relax into this new way of relating—don't rush her. Keep connecting to her and one day, she will start speaking to you, loud and clear.

Please note that even if you no longer have a physical womb, you can continue to connect to her energy—this will always be within you.

ABOUT THE AUTHOR

Emmi Mutale is an intuitive womb healer and energy medicine practitioner, dedicated to re-awakening ancient feminine wisdom. She works with women one-on-one and in groups with the intention of raising the frequency of our planet and fostering healing one womb at a time. Emmi creates sacred, safe, and non-judgmental spaces for deep healing and transformation and facilitates the emergence of authentic connection, profound knowing and inner power for women of all ages around the world.

Founder of *Feminine Revered*, Emmi also hosts the Sacred Feminine Power podcast, is a bestselling co-author of *Fearless Presence: Embodying Your Essence For Soul-Aligned Success*, and runs House of Gaia, a suburban sanctuary and a centre for healing and transformation in Lusaka, Zambia. With an MA in Human Rights, Emmi is dedicated to women's and child rights and is an advocate for health freedom.

Website: *www.femininerevered.com*
Facebook: *www.facebook.com/FeminineRevered*
Email: *emmi@femininerevered.com*

ESTHER LEMMENS

"The only way to deal with an unfree world is to become so absolutely free that your very existence is an act of rebellion." - Albert Camus

As I bumbled through my home city of Norwich earlier this week, enjoying the sunshine and really savouring what felt like the first warmer day of the year, I discovered a new tea shop.

I was welcomed with tasty samples and brewing demonstrations, and I said 'yes' to pretty much everything they offered me. My taste buds danced with delight as they experienced new subtle yet rich flavours and the unexpected creaminess of the oat milk matcha latte, which I've affectionately started calling 'comfort in a cup.'

I had already ventured out today (leaving the house once a day is more than enough for me), and when I got home, it was blustery and had started to rain. This is usually an excellent excuse to get (and stay) cosy indoors, but there was something in me that whispered, 'go.' I was wise enough to listen; I've learned to pay attention to those soft, joyful, intuitive nudges.

I managed to get to the tea shop before the weather got too fierce, and I decided to enjoy my choice of blend there, rather than taking it for a

walk. A handful of people came and went. Then a person came in. I got...
vibes. A sense of recognition.

They ordered their drink of choice and were very specific about the amount and proportion of the ingredients. It made me smile; I appreciate that in people. It was a customised concoction, and they invited the staff to sample it along with them, which they seemed to be used to. Then they turned to me and asked me if I'd like to try it, too. As if I needed persuading.

They took a seat next to me. There was a natural, friendly comfort, and a lovely conversation started.

In the past few years, having had many conversations with gender-diverse folks (for my podcast as well as socially), I've learned incredible, heart-warming, and mind-expanding things. One of those things is that our perception of how a person presents to the world does not necessarily reflect their gender identity.

I'm not just talking about the colour or type of clothes people wear, or the length and style of their hair, or whether they wear make-up or nail varnish. It also includes mannerisms; the subtle body language that is subconscious for most of us, and of course, their bodies.

We assume that someone we perceive to have a 'male' body = a man, and someone we perceive to have a 'female' body = a woman. But that's all it is—an assumption. And sometimes that assumption is wrong.

This person had a deep voice. They had facial hair. Most people wouldn't think twice and assume that this person was 'just a guy.' I'm able to detach myself from those assumptions more and more now; to keep that space open, with an energy of curiosity.

As we chatted about all sorts of delightful things, I mentioned I had a podcast about gender, and that I'm dating a trans woman. They paused for a moment. I could see them considering whether or not to voice their thoughts, and if my ears were safe to receive it.

"I guess I can tell you this then. I've been suffering with gender dysphoria for many years."

As I felt my heart open with compassion for their struggle, I also felt delighted that they chose to share this intimate detail of their life with me

—and the intuitive nudge to venture out despite the weather suddenly clicked into place, too.

I find it a real privilege when people allow me a glimpse into their inner world; when they are vulnerable and open. It's a brave thing to do, and a beautiful thing to be on the receiving end of. I honour and cherish it. It doesn't tend to happen often (not in the least because I'm a raging introvert) but since having conversations for my podcast, it has been a more regular occurrence.

They went on to say they wanted to transition, eventually. They were figuring things out; deciding what step to take first. The disheartening dilemma of the ever-growing NHS Gender Identity Clinic waiting list and not having the funds to go down the faster, private route. Wanting to change their name but concerned about disrespecting their parents for that gift bestowed. How different things might be had they started their transition earlier.

"Just so you're aware, the shop is closing soon." One of the staff members approached us reluctantly, trying not to interrupt our conversation. We gathered our things and made our way outside, the wind and rain a stark contrast with the warm cosiness of the shop.

"Christine."[1]

There was a casual matter-of-factness and yet a hint of hesitation as she spoke her new name to me. Her face lit up as she said it, and I caught a spark of something.

Her chosen name.

I got a sense she was still growing into it, like a much-coveted item of clothing that feels so right, yet too much to claim.

There was no doubt we would stay in touch.

Although I enjoy hugs, I don't necessarily like hugging just anyone—and I'm often reluctant to initiate it because I feel awkward. But I didn't want to leave without offering Christine a hug. She accepted.

I notice more and more how people feel safe to open up to me. I have no doubt it's a reflection of being more vulnerable and open with myself. Of honouring and cherishing *myself*, which has been the most painful and challenging journey I've ever been on, and yet I wouldn't trade it for anything. (Which, interestingly, seems to be an underlying thread of the stories people share with me about their gender journeys.)

Christine's story was unique, yet so familiar.

I believe we all have a deep desire to be our true selves and share this with the world. To be seen; to be heard; to be fully received. But when that differs from the norm, we risk being criticised, ridiculed, or threatened. *We feel unsafe.*

I also believe that a lot of our assumptions about others (and ourselves) are learned, and rooted in patriarchal conditioning; gender roles being one of these. We have internalised this, which causes us to police each other (and ourselves) to conform to these standards. When we encounter someone who does not conform, we experience this as a threat. *We feel unsafe.*

Talk about a clash.

I think that safety (or the lack of it) shapes a lot of our identity. It's part of the foundations. When you grow up without that, the roots of shame take its place. By the time we reach adulthood, most of us have some weeding to do.

As a child, I kept to myself a lot of the time. I often felt misunderstood. An outsider. Never quite fitting in. For years, I thought fitting in was what I wanted, but I've been learning that I mistook that for a desire to belong.

But how does one find belonging? It had always felt out of reach for me, and with this new and budding awareness, it suddenly seemed insurmountable.

It was like a fog slowly lifted; like trying to look out a window that's been steamed up for as long as I can remember. As more and more patches started to clear, I was shocked to see all the baggage I had shoved in the back of the closet and forgotten about. It was old and dusty and mouldy, and I knew it couldn't stay anymore. It was covering my light and hindering my life force.

Something dawned on me.

I'm not the person I thought I was.

I started to see all the ways in which I had rejected myself. Criticised and judged myself. Downright betrayed myself. Throughout my life. *My whole life.* I had opened Pandora's baggage and there was no closing it now. There it was, exposed and ugly.

My relationships were co-dependent. I lacked healthy communication skills. My emotional maturity was at the beginner level. I was a complete people pleaser and had no idea what my needs even were, let alone how to ask for them to be met. My boundaries were fuzzy at best, I avoided conflict at all costs, and perfectionism kept that inner critic alive and well.

I lived my life feeling like I was either too much or not enough.

I learned that these were coping strategies that originated in my childhood, when they helped keep me safe. I was bullied as a kid, and being highly sensitive (and probably neurodivergent), it affected me more than I ever realised. I got accustomed to performing strength and toughness; I couldn't let them see they got to me. Once or twice, I felt brave and stood up for myself, which resulted in severe retaliation. I learned to not rock the boat. I learned to make myself invisible.

These coping mechanisms accompanied me throughout my life, even though they didn't serve me anymore. *How do you make your voice heard to share your unique self-expression when all you've experienced is that it's not safe?*

Something inside me told me to slow down, to breathe, take a step back, and look at what felt like a complete mess of a life. What else did I dare see?

That I had become this emotional chameleon who had forgotten her true colours.

That I had gotten into the habit of pushing people away for fear of being abandoned or rejected, which stopped me from having the intimate connections and relationships I so longed for.

That this harsh inner voice is not really mine; it's the voice of the patriarchy. And it tells lies.

The foundations of my identity were shaken to the core, and I could do nothing but stand by and watch helplessly as they crumbled. And I knew that the only way to rebuild them was by deeply and completely accepting myself first. And fuck, that was challenging—*is* challenging.

Who even *was* I underneath all that rubble? What was my truth?

I considered what I'd been learning from my podcast guests. I approach them with curiosity and openness. What would happen if I applied this to myself?

I realised that a big step into this curious self-inquiry began just under ten years ago, when I met a trans non-binary person who would become my partner. I was bisexual, and here was this person who was not 'following the rules' about how to be a man or woman.

An inevitable internal shift was about to happen. Because I had feelings for this person who was breaking the binaries? No. Because *I was a bisexual person*. I *knew myself to be* bisexual. Although 'bisexual' means being attracted to two *or more* genders (and they don't even have to include the binary ones), to me at the time, it meant being attracted to men and women.

Something needed an upgrade. But what? I found two distinct parts. One, the label itself may need to change if I concluded it didn't feel resonant anymore. And two, I had to let go of my attachment to it. I had integrated this little word, this label, as a part of my identity, and it turned out a part of me had real trouble letting it go—or rather, letting it evolve. I was certain I would find more labels I got too attached to.

I learned the term 'pansexual', which means being attracted to people regardless of their gender. It felt right and more inclusive to me. Like the term 'queer,' which I also use for myself, I realised that rather than it being something new I learned about who I am, it simply provided new language to express a facet of who I've always been.

In the past few years, I've been meeting and getting to know a lot of gender-diverse folks, and I have found a sense of belonging in the queer community. In a brainstorming session with my project partner some years ago, when the Fifty Shades books were all the rage, another book idea was born: *Let's create a book with fifty stories of local gender non-conforming people, to show how much diversity there is in just one place! Fifty Shades of Gender!!*

Since we were not short on ideas, it got shelved for a few years. Then at the end of 2018, it started popping into my head again. And again. And again.

I recognise this pattern. It means something needs my attention.

Unfortunately, I am also quite prone to overthinking. I thought, "how would I even *start* this?" Queue brain overload and overwhelm.

"By taking one step," was the answer I got in those rare moments when I managed to soothe my mind. That step was a single conversation. Anything more felt too much; too big.

I asked a friend if they'd be willing to have a chat with me for the book. I would record it, have it transcribed, and turn it into a book chapter. After we had our conversation, I was struck by divine inspiration that said, *why not use the audio?* And so, the idea for the podcast was born.

I kept putting one foot in front of the other, and fast forward to the time of writing this, my podcast (also called Fifty Shades of Gender) is 21 months old and has seventy-five episodes. I'm not sure what has been more rewarding: the part of it that is going out into the world or the part of it that touched (and keeps touching) my inner world. It's a beautiful thing to notice the two are inseparable.

As the number of conversations I had with all these incredible people added up, I got more and more curious about gender. What exactly *is* this?

The more I learned, the less I understood it, and the more questions it raised. I remember when one of my podcast guests (in episode 34) asked, *"when you look inside yourself for your gender identity, what do you find?"*

I had to admit, I couldn't find anything.

Mind blown.

As it turned out, it was difficult to question gender without questioning *my own* gender.

If I found no gender inside of me, what *did* I find? I was born with these genitals, and based on that, someone assigned me the label 'woman.' This then caused me to be socialised in a particular way, which caused me to have certain experiences…

That's as far as I got.

I used to start my episodes by asking my guests, "What does it mean to you to be [insert gender identity]?" So I decided to ask myself, "what does it mean to me to be a woman?"

I discovered that the experiences I had as I was growing up—those things that were considered 'normal,' things we laughed off, things we were told to just get over or ignore—were laden with misogyny. Sexism. Oppression. How did I not see this before?! And not only did I believe the lies I was fed, but I had also become an active participant in perpetuating them.

I wanted to reject it all; to eject it into the ether. I started uncovering this dormant anger. I wanted to fight. Rebel. Resist. Be against.

"All feelings are for feeling," said Glennon Doyle, as I listened to the audiobook of *Untamed*. It was a revelation; I realised I had suppressed difficult emotions for as long as I could remember.

I let it all move through me. Powerlessness. Regret. Resentment. And pure, unadulterated rage.

I let it all burn.

As the fire waned into glowing embers, I understood that my soul guided me to start this podcast to help me heal, and when I say heal, I mean *I am healing*. It's an ongoing process.

One thing I've learned from my podcast guests is that (some) trans people transition not to become someone else; they transition to become more of themselves. Who they really are, and who they've probably always been. They want everything about them to reflect this; to be more at home within themselves.

I realised my own transformation had a similar essence at its core; to shed everything that is not me. To let more of myself shine. To come home to myself.

I still don't know what it means to me to be a woman. But I do feel an affinity with womanhood, and I will keep refining and redefining it for myself. Because even though there is a collective experience of 'womanhood,' there is no one way to be a woman—just like there is no one way to be a man, or trans, or non-binary, or any other gender.

Every woman experiences womanhood differently. For some, this includes being a parent; for others, it doesn't. For some, it includes femininity; for others, it doesn't. The possibilities are endless.

Maybe I'm simply a human with a woman experience.

I'm also a human with a Dutch experience. With an immigrant experience. With an empath experience. An intuitive experience. A podcaster, artist, writer experience. And so many more.

And as unique as our experiences are, there's one thing we have in common: We're all souls with a human experience.

How can we be free in an oppressive system? Is that even possible?

I believe so. For me, the answer is to stay curious and open-minded. To keep rediscovering, unlearning, and deconditioning. To continue to redesign myself in response to that inner guidance. To trust, respect and honour myself. To treat myself as sacred. To belong to myself. To love myself as much as I possibly can.

Self-love is a radical act; perhaps the most radical of all. And *that* is what the world needs most right now.

---

1. Name used with permission.

ABOUT THE AUTHOR

Esther (she/they) is a creator, artist, budding writer, podcaster, intuitive, truth seeker, and gentle activist. Generally non-conforming, she likes to refer to herself as a 'rebel with a cause.' Her motto is "do YOUR thing, YOUR way," and she passionately believes that authentic, unapologetic and at times radical self-expression is the most important gift we can give to ourselves—and to the world.

Esther is the founder and host of the *Fifty Shades of Gender* podcast. She is also queer, pansexual, non-monogamous, and dedicated to being the best gender-diverse ally she can be. She was nominated for the 2021 Positive Role Model Award (LGBT+) in the National Diversity Awards.

Esther moved to the UK from her native Netherlands in 1999 and is a graphic designer by profession. In her free time, she enjoys drinking tea, stroking cats, hugging trees, and spending time with her squish.

Websites: *www.estherlemmens.com*
www.fiftyshadesofgender.com
www.zesty.me

18

GEORGINA EL MORSHDY

THE ART OF REDESIGNING THE WORLD BY BEING MORE YOU

"Speak your mind, even if your voice shakes." - Maggie Kuhn

I **knew I wanted to write a chapter for this book the moment I saw the title.**

To me, the idea of a sacred redesign feels super potent in light of the challenges humanity faces in these times. Looking around, it's clear we didn't build a world that works for most people. Instead, western culture has built systems and structures that prioritise profit, creating a world where people and the planet come second.

I often wonder if humanity has arrived at the crossroads of *evolution or extinction.*

As we head into a perfect storm of complex issues, I'm sure Mother Nature *will* survive. I don't believe it's our job to *'save the world'* because the earth has the power to regenerate herself. For me, the closer truth is the need to save humanity and prove we deserve to call this one-in-a-million planet 'home'.

The stakes for this collective mission couldn't be higher. Our individual and collective actions today will decide what kind of world our children and grandchildren inherit—if any.

But despite all the dark predictions and what-if scenarios, I choose to believe humanity *will* find a way. Sure, the clock is ticking, but the future is still unwritten.

And maybe we were born for these times...

I believe each of us incarnated with a unique mission and gift that can help elevate our collective consciousness at this pivotal time in our history.

At times, I wonder if this vision is just wishful thinking!

What can I do? I'm just one person. How can I possibly do anything that would make a meaningful difference—especially given the colossal scale of issues we face.

I check myself when these doubts bubble up because I don't want to spark a self-fulfilling prophecy. If you believe action is pointless, there's zero motivation to change. Worst still, you might bury your head in the sand and hope that problems will disappear. If we adopt inertia as a collective, we'll prove ourselves right. NOTHING will change. We'll reinforce the status quo and keep creating more of the same chaos.

In comparison, if we choose to live through the lens of hope and possibility, cultivating self-leadership and the belief that each of us has the power to inspire change, we can activate a growing confidence that a new path is possible.

This thought excites me because it means we don't need to wait for the top-down approach alone. In fact, I'm unconvinced the current hierarchy holds the new paradigm vision humanity needs. After all, this hierarchy is intrinsically woven into the existing power structures that create and maintain the status quo.

Instead, I believe seismic change will come from a grassroots crescendo of 'ordinary' people offering their gifts, inherent genius, and uniqueness, in community and collaboration.

As Helen Keller said, *"Alone we can do so little; together we can do so much."*

In other words, what if the change humanity desires starts with YOU?

And if that's the case, how do we fulfil this destiny?

∽

"Knowing yourself is the beginning of all wisdom." - Aristotle.

I was blessed to have a true matriarch as a grandparent. Ephra was a one-of-a-kind woman who left an indelible mark on your heart. She was my rock and my constant support. I love her so much.

I'll forever treasure the incredible conversation my cousin and I had with her towards the end of her life. I remember asking, *"Grandma, what piece of life advice do you want to leave me?"*

Her answer was two simple but powerful words—*KNOW THYSELF.*

On the surface, this is one of those throwaway statements that you're tempted to nod at and say, *"yeah, yeah, I know that..."*

Sure, we know our names and our occupations. We know what we like, and we can talk about all the things that turn us off.

We know all the surface, easy-to-access things!

But in a world of information abundance and fast-moving social timelines, I fear we're increasingly disconnected from the depth of who we are.

And it's a BIG problem...

In a world, where the human attention span is now officially less than a goldfish's, attention and the ability to navigate depth are powerful skills.

How long can you sit with something?
How much complexity can you hold?
How much detail are you willing to navigate?

The answers are always within.

The more we can explore an inner journey, the more capacity we create for ourselves and for life. In turn, the more ideas, answers, and solutions we can uncover.

Who we are at the surface pales in comparison to the mysteries inside.

Deep inside each of us lies a voice of unconditional love that KNOWS it's intricately connected to *everything*. Therefore it sees others as divine beings—not commodities to be exploited or monetised.

This same part understands that it moves in a body built with borrowed components from the earth. Therefore, it has a deep reverence and respect for the earth—because it's of the earth.

This essence also knows it's connected to God, Source, the Universe (or whatever words you resonate with). Through this connection, it can access intuition, channel divine guidance, and discern Individual Wisdom.

The truth is we *always* know what's right for us—and for the world—because we are loved and guided by consciousness.

If we tap in...

Imagine... What if the most radical thing we can do as individuals in these pivotal times is to be MORE of who we already are (and who we incarnated to be)?

What if our greatest service to the world is intrinsically linked to the most profound knowledge of our truth... And our ability to express that truth fearlessly?

What if knowing our truth is the catalyst for remembering the change we incarnated to spark?

This is why I love inspiring people to step into their inner labyrinth and get curious about all the nooks and crannies of their souls. I'm obsessed with activating the courage it takes to worship our internal landscape and map it in the same way we would a new place of discovery.

I believe that who you are,
What you've experienced,
What you know,
And what you can do is enough to light a match of possibility.

Once lit, your match holds the power to ignite a fire of change.

How far your individual fire spreads depends on who's in your circle.
Who resonates with what you have to say.
And what other fires connect up with yours.

In other words, your YOU has the power to change the world.

Imagine the change we'd spark if every human stepped into their most authentic self and embraced their unique role on this planet.

Fearless visible dancers, writers, gardeners, orators, leaders, inventors, visionaries, creatives, entrepreneurs, artists, performers, and commentators—to name just a few—all infusing their unique blend of magic into this world.

I think the impact would be seismic. Our uniqueness is that potent, but this shouldn't be a surprise. Nature also models this truth. Where monoculture is devoid of biodiversity, a natural ecosystem is alive with thousands of species collaborating, co-existing, and interacting to create a self-sustaining, regenerative environment.

The human ecosystem could be the same—if we cultivate the courage to be MORE of who we came here to be.

For example, my daughter is an incredible singer-songwriter. I urge her to share her talent because her voice, expressed through her unique lens on the world, will activate and move a particular group of people.

Her authentic presence makes a massive difference.

As does yours—because there are people in the world *right now* who need to receive your unique blend of magic. If they receive it from anyone else, it won't resonate as deeply or as completely for the sole reason that they are NOT you.

This makes the inner work to know yourself and express your truth one of the most potent actions you can take to benefit humanity.

I get if this pathway to a sacred redesign sounds too simple.

But know this...

The Inner Journey followed by a desire to be more YOU is both confronting and uncomfortable as well as liberating, cathartic, and paradigm-shaping.

～

"Don't be satisfied with stories, how things have gone with others. Unfold your own myth." - Rumi

Inner work holds up an ever-present mirror of self-reflection where you can no longer look away from the truth of who you are.

On the upside, you have an invitation to see, own, and use all the gifts and talents you've previously underplayed, undervalued, and down-right ignored.

On the downside, you'll be invited to confront the pain, shame, trauma, anger, etc. that you harbour due to a lifetime of being human in a paradigm that prioritises profit over people and the planet.

As you dive deeper, you'll realise that you can't ever truly escape yourself!

And through that truth, you get to learn to love yourself which means no more numbing or escaping. No more bypassing uncomfortable experiences.

No more trying to fit in in a way that isn't you either.

No more pretending to be something or someone you're not.

Or pasting on a social mask because you think it makes you more beautiful.

No more shying away from expressing the words on your lips.

No more hiding your truth, your beliefs, your passion.

Instead, the choice to do inner work creates an invitation to live AUTHENTICALLY. It connects you with your true gifts so you can spend more time doing what you love while being someone that you love.

In the process, you help shift the needle for humanity by saying the things only you can say, and doing the things only you can do.

These benefits sound fantastic, but there's a flip side.

You *will* be judged for your truth. That's inevitable.
You'll be criticised too.
And ridiculed.
Doubted.
Shamed.
Rejected.
Denied.

Some people won't like you (and often, they won't even know why). Some people won't be able to handle you. Others won't believe you or will be too triggered by what you have to say and who you really are.

In comparison, there will be those people who will hang on to your every word. They'll be inspired to make moves in their own lives because your voice and example give them the permission to do so. They'll see you as a leader and will observe your embodiment as a signal of what they want to integrate for themselves.

You have to be OK navigating this duality. You have to develop the emotional capacity to manage the spectrum of feelings and experiences that arise when you choose to be more YOU.

You'll also have to be OK with what fearless visibility can cost you.

For example, your authenticity might cost you a client.
Or a gig.
Or a dream opportunity.
Or a partner.
Or money.
Or the validation.
Or the recognition.
Or the external love or acceptance.

But as you release things that aren't aligned with your truth, you create space to receive the things that are. For me, this experience has looked like more aligned clients. It's looked like receiving money to navigate the current paradigm from places I didn't expect. It's meant unexpected opportunities, which turned out to be exactly what I needed to serve humanity at higher and higher levels.

In addition, you become more deeply rooted in the truth of who you are, creating more and more magic.

~

"Go inward to create more power outward."

There are many paths to knowing yourself.

I believe one of the most potent tools you can leverage for this journey is journaling.

Journaling is a practice that takes you beyond the surface into the depths of who you are. In turn, you unlock vast amounts of space for hypothesising, questioning, contemplating, and imagining. In the privacy of your journal, you get to follow the threads of your thinking and feeling to uncover new connections, new ideas, and new ways of doing old things.

Journaling is an opportunity to have a two-way conversation with yourself. As you play the role of the observer and the writer, you get to dig deep, unravel the thoughts and ideas that meander through your soul, and capture your true essence on paper.

As you express your heart, you'll discover insights, gifts, and a calling so potent you'll feel compelled to step up and be more you.

You'll also discover a beautiful correlation…

The more you know yourself, the easier it gets to be fearlessly visible with the truth you came here to share.

Here are some tips for meaningful journaling.

1. DON'T CENSOR YOURSELF.

This first point is super important. We often censor ourselves because we worry about what others might think of us. We fear judgement, and we want to fit in.

Let your journal be that safe space where you're free to EXPRESS yourself fully.

Your journal can be the place where you can get things off your chest. You can vent. Say the 'silly' things. Write down the stuff you'd never say out loud.

Remember, you can destroy your writing afterwards. No one needs to see what you've written. You don't even need to read it back. The act of expressing how you feel in the moment is cathartic and even liberating. Give yourself permission to really go there—and see what unfolds.

2. WATCH THE INNER CRITIC.

It's always there! Hovering over your shoulder and ready to step in!!

Remember, the intention with journaling isn't to write something that you'll later publish (although you might). Therefore it doesn't matter if your spelling is terrible. You don't need to structure your writing in any logical order. You can bounce all over the place—just like your thoughts and feelings do.

It's more important to NOTICE and ACKNOWLEDGE 'truth' than to write perfection.

Be warned! The inner critic doesn't just show up to criticise the quality of your writing. It will happily judge the content and context too! When your critic makes an appearance, thank it and tell it you're OK.

Heighten your ability to notice any urge to censor or deny yourself.

Then get back to writing whatever needs to be expressed, revealed, and released—in whatever format that might take. Sink into the art of acknowledging what's really happening for you because that's where the true magic lies.

3. EXPLORE JOURNALING PROMPTS.

Prompts are ideal if you want to journal, but are stumped by the blank page. A good question makes it easy to move through writer's block because your mind will almost certainly generate an answer.

Enjoy exploring these powerful journaling prompts as you journey closer to your YOU.

1. What's your personal hope for humanity?
2. What do you want your children and grandchildren to say about you?
3. What has your life taught you about how to live a 'good' life? How could you incorporate more of these teachings into your work?
4. What do you do so naturally, that you can struggle to appreciate its true value?
5. How can you incorporate more of this gift into your work and everyday life to expand your impact and serve at a higher level?
6. What scares you most about being a voice for positive change?
7. What can you let go so it's easier to be more fearlessly visible with your truth?
8. How could you live in a way that expands your YOU every single day?

Our inner world holds our unique calibration point and soul blueprint for serving humanity.

This is why one of *the* most powerful things we can do right now is to find our YOU, know our truth, and get fearlessly visible with the gifts we incarnated to share.

Do the inner work. Dive into your journal. Commit to knowing yourself at ever deeper levels. Invite depth, seek out answers, and cultivate the presence to hear your soul speak.

Chances are, you'll uncover a depth of magic and mystery that will give you confidence in your voice as a vessel for change and sacred redesign.

When we embrace the power of our uniqueness, it's easy to sink into the work we came here to do. The path of YOU allows each of us to make a difference through the things that are so intrinsically part of who we are, that we sometimes doubt their value.

This is how your YOU holds the potential to change the world.

As a Hillel The Elder once said, *"If not now, when? If not you, who?"*
It's time to get to work.
Our children are watching.
Here's to more YOU.

Georgina.

ABOUT THE AUTHOR

Georgina El Morshdy is the founder of Find Your YOU and the creator of the Aligned Message Activator. She's a messaging mentor, an intuitive writer, a creative muse, and the host of the Writing Your Best Self podcast.

Georgina is passionate about using message-making as a catalyst for personal growth and a tool for sparking impact. She believes that in these changing times, our individuality is one of the most potent tools we have for living a fully expressed life while making a positive difference in the world.

Through her programs, private coaching, and journaling tools, Georgina empowers impact-driven entrepreneurs, creatives, and visionaries to activate and amplify their unique voice, vision, and visibility - so they can *surface, shape and share* their soul's message for impact, income, and influence.

Georgina lives in Plymouth, UK, with her three children and husband. When she's not message-making, she loves journaling, creating with her singing bowls, long walks by the ocean, and deep conversations that touch your soul.

Website: *www.findyouryou.co.uk/sacred-redesign*
Facebook: *www.facebook.com/georgina.morshdy*
Podcast: *www.writingyour.bestself.co*

19

JENNIFER SPOR

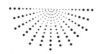

For the better part of my current life, I've believed in destiny. That is, that fate is what you're born into, but destiny is how you choose to shape your circumstances.

I say "better part" because up until I was 16, that wasn't the case. Up until then, I would describe my childhood as a collection of fragmented memories. Years of abuse sexually, emotionally, physically, and mentally were suppressed at a conscious level that served as a coping mechanism to survive. It wouldn't be until much later in my life that many of those memories would come back into my awareness to be healed and crystallized into wisdom, equipping me for the work I'm doing now.

I have memories of abuse as far back as infancy. The earliest memory is of my biological father picking me up by my neck and swinging me around a room. I must have been under a year old, and I only know that because my mom took me and left him when I was around 1, never to see him again. She was also pregnant at the time with my sister who she would give up for adoption at birth. My mom could never really tell me much about this time as I sensed that she had a lot of suppressed unhealed trauma, but I had a knowing that she had to have wanted my sister to have a better life than what she felt she could provide.

My mom and I were on our own for a few years until she met my younger sister's father when I was 4 or 5. Many of the memories I have from that time were of feeling alone as even when my mom was with me it didn't really feel like she was with me. She eventually remarried, and my younger sister came into the world when I was 6. Just a couple months after my sister was born, my stepfather committed suicide. That in of itself is a story but suffice to say after that my mom became even more checked out. My mom was never doting but even as a young child, I could sense she lost part of her soul that night.

Fast forward a few years later, I was 11 and that's when things at home started escalating. I began to push back with my mom because I was often home alone caring for my 5-year-old sister, and I resented her for not being around and when she was she wasn't mentally or emotionally available. Being with her was unpredictable. Some days she would call me names, tell me she wished I'd never been born, physically restrain me, or throw things at me. My solution for this was running away and turning to alcohol to numb out when I was 12.

I was in and out of my mom's house until I was 14. I was living with a friend at the time and we weren't getting along. I was home alone in her house a lot and that combined with the trauma I'd experienced up to that point along with the alcohol abuse led me to a very dark place. At 14, I tried to take my own life. I spent a month in a children's psych ward and then landed back at home with my mom. I pleaded with the therapist not to make me leave with her. I'd felt my cry for help fell on deaf ears.

Two more years of living at home would pass, and during that time, I attribute my survival to being out of the home as much as possible. Often I would be working or looking for other excuses to be away from home… until one day I snapped.

I confided in relatives asking if I could come and live with them but they said no. So I waited until my mom left the home one morning, packed up as many of my things that I could take with me and left to live in another town. I didn't tell her where I was, and I never went back.

That was the day I made a decision that I was going to survive and that I wanted more for my life.

I made a decision that I would shape my own destiny.

Over the next 2 years, I worked full time to support myself. Despite my newfound independence, I was still drinking a lot and experimenting with drugs to numb the pain from the unhealed trauma.

When I was 18, I felt like I needed a fresh start, so I moved to Seattle. I started out working a few different jobs, and then at 19 years old, I landed in retail. A few months later, I had a conversation with myself that would change the trajectory of my life.

As far back as I could remember, I'd always wanted to be a teacher. I thought about what would be required to pursue a path in the traditional academic space, financially supporting myself, paying for college, etc. Then I reflected on where I was in my current job. I already really loved what I was doing in retail and decided that I was committed to creating a career in that industry.

I was on a mission. By the time I was 21, I was already managing stores. At 26, I went to work for a company that would recognize my potential, and I would eventually climb the ladder to assume a corporate director role at 32, overseeing store operations in over 1200 locations. I was the youngest director in my department then—and female. Back then, that was a big accomplishment in an environment that was still very much a good ol' boys club at that time.

For many years, I loved my career. What I loved the most was having the ability to create an impact for other people on such a large scale, to make a real difference in the lives of employees and customers.

Despite how much I loved my career in retail, it also demanded a lot of my energy, attention, and time. Over time, it felt more difficult to make a difference amidst a growing company with growing bureaucracy, and I fell out of love with my career.

Like so many others, I believed if I checked all of the boxes off of what traditional society programs us to believe it means to achieve success then I would be happy and fulfilled.

Despite everything I'd overcome and accomplished in my life I wasn't happy or fulfilled. I was exhausted, burned out, and I felt like an empty shell of a person.

I was living in the illusion that if I acquired all the things and that if others thought I was successful then I would be healed and that I would be whole.

That was when the fog started to lift.

That was the moment I started waking up.

Spiritual awakenings can happen instantaneously, but the awakening often unfolds over time because we as humans are also programmed to fear change so we resist.

Despite my realization about no longer wanting to be where I thought I would be until I retired, I took zero action.

Almost 2 more years would go by until I finally took action. I allowed my fear of change to cripple me mentally and emotionally. My unhealed trauma earlier in my life contributed greatly to that. I constantly worried about my ability to find another job such as the one I had without a college degree and making as much as I was at the time. I didn't feel good enough. Another illusion I was living in.

My catalyst for taking action was my mom. Yes, you read that right. We were estranged for years until my 20s. I didn't actually reconnect with her even then, but my sister kept in touch with her and would share where she was and what she was up to.

The first time I saw my mom, she was living in a motel. She'd lost a lot of weight and she didn't seem fully mentally present. I remember asking her if she wanted a soda from the vending machine. When she said yes, I walked around the corner and broke down in tears. I was crying for the unhealed child in me who had just seen her mother for the first time in so many years, and I was crying for my mom who looked so malnourished and unwell. It was clear she had experienced some type of mental break. I would later find out that she was diagnosed with a mental illness. That coupled with her own unhealed trauma would explain so much of what I'd experienced with her as a child. From that moment on my journey to forgiveness and healing began and we would keep in touch.

It wasn't witnessing my mom in the state she was in that propelled me into action to leave my career. It was a few years later after she was diagnosed with stage 4 lung cancer that I reached my breaking point.

During that time, I was traveling back and forth from the east coast to the northwest to be with my mom and my family as much as possible. Just days before my mom transitioned, I was at her bedside, and my phone was blowing up. There was an issue at work that in the realm of everything wasn't the most important thing at the time and the issue could have been prevented like so many other "fires" that I had to put out in my director role. I was being faced with the decision of directing my attention toward this issue or being present for my mom who was dying. It was in that moment that I broke. I made the decision that I would no longer allow myself to be stuck in my own life and that I was taking my power back. That was the beginning of the end of my career in retail.

In that moment, my courage exceeded my fear, and I vowed to myself to create a life on my own terms where I was happy, fulfilled, and free.

After my mom died, I wanted to be closer to my family in Idaho. Much like the storyline of a country song, I rented my house in New Jersey, packed up my car, and headed out west.

After all of what I'd realized and this awakening I was experiencing, I was still living in denial. At first, when I moved, I thought finding a new job would solve my problem with feeling stagnant in my career. Wrong!

God has a way of redirecting us. I'd aced several interviews with some well-known retail companies, positions I was a shoo-in for. In each instance, there would be a strange reason why the position didn't work out. One time I was even interviewed by a company six times, flown out to meet their team, and the opportunity still fell through. It was after that I finally realized I wasn't meant to continue the work I was doing and that put me in a place of reflection about what could be next.

It was this time of reflection that led me to the decision to create a whole new path as an entrepreneur. Throughout my journey of awakening to my spiritual path and all of the life transitions I was experiencing, I invested in spiritual teachers, readings, therapy, healers, and business coaches but there wasn't anyone I could find that could support me in bringing it all together to integrate who I was becoming into my physical reality. This is what led me to realize my purpose and the mission I'm meant to fulfill supporting others in aligning with their highest path.

Today I live my purpose and mission through my business as an Akashic Records Channel, Soul-Led Business Mentor, and Strategist for high achieving spiritual leaders who are feeling called to step into their next level of expansion in their purpose and mission. Spiritual leaders aren't just in the personal development industry. There are healers, visionaries, teachers, coaches, and creatives in every industry and those yet to be known to us. Innovators who know they are answering a higher calling and forging a new path for others to follow.

We are living in a time where many are being guided to birth new creations that support our evolution. Listening and taking action on the purpose and mission that God has placed in your heart is an absolute necessity for navigating the path forward.

If you are reading this, there's a reason.

You know you're meant for more. Your soul is bringing forward the next level YOU to be expressed. Whether you're newly discovering your purpose and mission or you're being called to step into the next level of your evolution, the time is now.

I know. Intellectually understanding this, feeling called, and integrating that into your physical reality can feel easier said than done.

Here is how you can move forward:

1. *Drop into your heart space for reflection and decision-making.* The heart is the intersection of the spiritual and physical; it is where you're soul's guidance resides.

The mind is a faithful servant but it will always make decisions based on what it knows from conditioning and past experience therefore it will always keep you where you are. Your soul will always guide you toward expansion, which is often an unknown path, but the most aligned path for your growth.

2. *Get clear on your values, strengths, gifts, and what brings you the most JOY.* Even if you've done this in the past it can change over time. Your journey here is an evolution! Your purpose and the mission you're here to fulfill will include all of these and provide clarity on your path forward.

3. *Set clear intentions.* Visualize your path to the extent that you can see and feel what it's like to embody the version of yourself who is living your highest purpose and mission.

4. *Create a strategy that supports the manifestation of your vision.* Decide when you want to realize your vision and create a plan that backs into that timeframe.

5. *Take aligned action.* Your strategy, how you spend your time, the actions you take, relationships, and mindset all need to align with your vision for the most direct path to achieve what you desire.

6. *Invest in support.* Your journey is evolutionary and you only know what you know. You may be able to figure things out on your own eventually but having objective support will help you achieve your goals a lot faster. We all have blind spots and having the support of someone who has experienced and achieved where you want to be is priceless.

More than anything, believe in yourself and leap forward in faith. You wouldn't feel a calling or have a vision in your heart that you aren't already fully equipped to achieve.

You already have the answers. It's time to remember, to create space for the ancient wisdom already within you to come forward to be expressed.

Let go of who you were so that you can surrender to who you're meant to be.

You've been training for this for lifetimes. You are here to create heaven on earth.

ABOUT THE AUTHOR

Jennifer Spor is an Akashic Records Channel, Soul-Led Business Mentor, and Strategist for high-achieving Spiritual Leaders who are ready to step into the next level of expansion in living their purpose and fulfilling their mission. She also hosts the Awake & On Purpose podcast.

When she isn't in her business contributing to raising the consciousness of the planet she is out in nature and enjoying new adventures with her husband.

Website: www.jenniferspor.com
Email: jennifer@jenniferspor.com
LinkedIn: www.linkedin.com/in/jenniferspor

JOLYNN VAN ASTEN

"The only person who can solve the labyrinth of yourself is you." - Jeremy Denk

ENTER

As a youth, the beaches of the largest freshwater chain of lakes in the world are where I would find myself most summer months. The Eagle River Chain of Lakes, to be exact. Teeming with blue jays, cardinals, American crows, namesake eagles, noisy bullfrogs, MOSQUITOES, yet sparsely populated with humans. It didn't feel like my grandparents' cottage was underpopulated. Gatherings of the "family," the dogs, the alcohol.

I loved the shoreline. The rocks were large and smooth. The lake water seemed like a brown cola beverage. I'd take my plastic 1970s beach pail and shovel to gather wet sand and native mussels. Mussels intrigued me. I was curious about the creature inside. How did it build that shell? How did it survive? I'd converse with a few and believe I heard them tell me their lake-life adventures.

When my grandparents' sassy young Schnauzer Fritzie would waddle down and meet me at the shore, I'd quickly return the mussels. He and I would sit in a quiet spot away from the noise of the cottage. Creativity flowed as we made many wet-sand baked goods to sell to the solitary sandpipers that would run past. Fritzie was my sweetest friend. He was plump like me and always seemed to be in trouble.

I missed him deeply during the Fall school days. I was constantly ridiculed for my weight, dreading being back home after the final announcements mumbled through the air. I was one of two girls on the street I lived on. The girl next door had developmental disabilities and was under verbal attack every time she'd leave her house. I steered clear from her as I was fighting my own battles. Immature, unsupervised boys found us both easy targets to have their way with.

We moved across town when I was in the fourth grade. I was emotionally numb by that point—the chronic abuse from the teenage neighbor boy had taken a toll on my soul. My imagination was still intact, and I would often pretend that I was the popular Barbara Eden character from the iconic *I Dream of Jeannie* television show. Escape to my plush, Arabian-chic hideaway, my inner-bottle, with purple velvet seating, golden embellishments, jewels, and flowing fabric was the perfect hideaway.

The new neighborhood came with a natural pond unharmed by the building of our new construction home, teeming with mallards, red-winged blackbirds, tadpoles, dragonflies, fish and tall common cattails. Finally, some beings who would "get me." I would spend every waking moment at its tiny shoreline, conversing and dreaming with these nonjudgmental friends. As soon as an ice cream container would be emptied, I'd take it to the pond and fill it with tadpoles and bring them to the garage and watch them grow. (Yes, I always returned them safely once they sprouted legs.)

I would lie in bed at night with a flashlight and a copy of *A Field Guide to Birds of North America* by Chandler S. Robbins. I would identify my backyard friends and memorize their unique vocalizations.

Another one of my favorite books to escape with was *Mrs. Frisby and The Rats of NIMH* by Robert C. O'Brien. I could escape to the world of Mrs. Frisby's dear home of a cinder block and her troubles. My deepest heart's desire, even at that tender age, was to be a mother. A *kind* mother, and Mrs. Frisby's care and concern for her family and her tenacity resonated with me deeply. (No matter what age you are currently if you haven't read this Newberry award-winning classic, now is the time!)

I believe some of us have that calling and know from small on that we are here to be mothers as part of our work on the earth.

FOLLOW THE PATH

I found a renewed hope for learning the year of the move thanks to my teacher, Cheryl Trapp, a vibrant 34-year-old with a hearty laugh and outfits that would have been perfect for a cruise on The Love Boat. If there would have been a Magic School Bus and a Ms. Frizzle at the time, it would have been her. Hands-on adventures, a winning smile, writing assignments that evoked imagination and explored personification. For the first time I couldn't wait to get to school.

That all changed on March 1, 1979. We all eagerly went to our desks, but there was no Ms. Trapp. There was a gentle, gray-haired woman at the front of the room with a somber look on her face. "Children, I have some sad news. Ms. Trapp was killed in a car accident last night."

I don't remember if we finished the day or were released early. I just know it was cold and dark as I walked the two miles from the school to my pond to tell the others what happened.

HELD

There was a special feel to the printed pages of magazines of the 1980s. One of eight at a large rectangular table in the middle of a high school art room, I flipped through stacks of magazines seeking inspiration for a two-dimensional pastel and charcoal drawing.

I was obsessed with drawing hands. Life-like, precise. I often drew my own. I would hold a Maybelline mascara or some other sacred trinket that emerged from my purse in my non-dominant hand while I sketched it out with my dominant hand.

Something about the walnut laminated table made my skin tones pop. I fantasized about being a hand model for beauty companies. My fingers were well-shaped, and my nails were usually coated in a clear pink polish.

This was a part of my body I found acceptable to reveal to the world. It was, to me, aesthetically pleasing and useful.

I noticed the boys at my table ripping out pages of cars, dirt bikes, and cigarettes. I chuckled because I loved to doodle cigarettes on all of my notebooks. I found the cylindrically shaped object simple to replicate, fun to shade, and interactive as I would smoke it in my imagination and doodle its disintegration in front of me.

Yes, I was the girl who would skip lunch and go across the schoolyard to smoke cigarettes. I unconsciously found them to be meditative and would spend many a cold night talking with Orion, Canis Major, and other heavenly friends while trying to soothe my nerves.

That day I was pleased with my hunt for inspiration. Before me were pages with sleek perfume bottles, nude women bent in ways that hid anything too revealing, flowers, orcas, seahorses, and timepieces.

My paper was toned tan with enough tooth to grab the pigment of the pastels. It was larger compared to the papers my tablemates chose to create with. Mine was a robust 24 x 36 inches. I placed it down and gave no thought to the fact that I was taking up more space than my cohorts.

At the time I didn't understand that it was my intuition flashing images in my mind that I would visually express, but it was. It was more than my imaging faculty, it was a precise vision flashing before me of the finished work. The paper was never blank or void to me. I would lay it in front of me, run my hands over it in awe and gratitude, each paper was my newest friend. Invaluable. In a flash I would see the finished work and reach out to my other close friend, the charcoal pencil, and start to sketch, proportionally accurate, and generally magnified.

I loved to hone in on an area, like a hand. I felt as though I was seeing through a mystic microscope, larger than life, focusing solely on what I was expressing, as though all of the world around it was non-existent. If it was a bottle, there was no reference to the shelf beneath it a statue, no sky above or ground below. Just a close-up of one area.

So that day the hand of what seemed to be an immortal feminine presence appeared before me. A mildly cupped hand, fingers turning up ever so slightly. If it was my own hand, it would have been my right hand. A direct side view, the thumb, its nail, the knuckles down, pointing toward the earth, the index finger gently curved, the tip of the middle, and the ring finger peeking through, no visible sign of the pinkie.

The valley of the palm was out of sight. However in the palm was a side view silhouette of a female sitting with her feet toward the fingers, her knees bent. Pulled in tight, she was completely folded, almost fetal like in nature, with her arms wrapped tightly around them, her head down. Her back was toward the wrist.

In the large female hand before me, proportionally she was like Fay Wray to King Kong in the classic 1933 version of the film. *She fit.*

Above her head, almost exploding out of the open palm were rainbows, trumpets, clocks, seahorses, stars, ribbons, planets, and more. Pure lifeforce energy, sound, *aliveness.* It almost seemed that the woman in the hand of the immortal being could not bear to look at the potent energy around her, even though the explosion of life seemed joyful. It was much safer to stay curled up.

That piece of art ended up being entered into a judged county art exhibit. I was the only youth, 15 at the time, who took a blue ribbon in a contest filled with seasoned fine artists.

"In all chaos there is a cosmos, in all disorder a secret order." - Carl Jung

TOWARD CENTER

Discouraged by my immediate family from pursuing art as a career, and with a high drive to escape the dysfunction that surrounded me, I surrendered to stepping into the dull world of the status quo. Persephone was officially in the underworld. The inherent sacred patterns of stargazer, artist, joy-seeker and other elements of my sacred design were still there, albeit now buried under layers of misery and discontent.

Carl Jung's quote rang true. A secret order did shine through the dark disorder as sparks of joy emerged. Five amazing children, three sons and two daughters. Each one arrived in what to the outside world may have seemed like terrible timing. To me, each one showed up in the labyrinth-like timeline of my life as perfectly positioned divine appointments. I still wanted nothing more than to be a mom.

Creativity helped us move through challenging times together in the form of homeschool projects. In the early days, you could find us reenacting crossing the Delaware, with our sofa as a boat. Sheets and blankets were placed atop tunnels of repurposed cardboard boxes to form a giant canal that we could crawl through. Not a journey to the center of the earth, that would be too ordinary. Rather a giant ear canal that led us to the bones of the middle ear.

Maps and timelines were plastered over every bit of available wall space so the children could visually process that Squanto lived concurrently with Shakespeare. We created together despite the rocky events that unfolded around us.

I would turn the winding turns within the labyrinth of my life that seemed like they would land my little clan in a longed-for calm space, only to find us out in the remote edges of the pattern, feeling lost.

I had the walk within the contemplative unicursal labyrinth confused with a never-ending maze. What I thought were walls and dead ends were gentle curves.

I would stop walking for what seemed like micro-eternities, believing we were stuck, and like Mrs. Frisby, that we were doomed to be plowed over in the field, and that our little cinder block home would be destroyed. I didn't know there were mighty unseen helpers that could safely redirect us.

LISTENING

"You will seek me and find me when you seek me with all your heart." - (English Standard Version, Jeremiah 29:13)

Meditation and prayer became a non-negotiable daily staple as I sought to bring the fruits of Creativity and Peace back into my life. Slowly, buds appeared, blooms came forth. I quieted my mind and began to not just incessantly inquire to the heavens, rather I engaged in listening. Listening and discerning between the voice in my head and the voice of God.

Clear direction emerged and the lines of the path in the "labyrinth" proved useful as I headed toward and found *The Center*. Intentional redesign, a full transformation of my conditioned mind, while walking out the path now became a vital conscious choice. The inquiry became, "What is the Sacred plan? What is mine to do? Who am I here to serve, my children yes...and?"

The internally downloaded images that my spirit nature would receive so bright and intuitively as a youth began returning, but now through a meditative time of communication personally between me and the Lord. Through meditation, sacred inquiry, and intuitive expression through visual journaling, the cobwebs of my mind began to clear away. The open wounds within my heart and soul naturally healed.

CENTER

Rather than exiting *The Center* quickly after discovering it, I would linger there, accessing and absorbing the peace that flowed throughout my body like a true healing elixir. *The Center* was portable to me. I didn't have to be on my seated cushion, or near a certain birch tree. I could be anywhere on the earth and also be in *The Center*. I learned that *The Center* was now a state of being that I occupy with my attention. I learned that the more I familiarized myself with its vibrations, its tones, I could receive next steps, clear direction, and insights.

I heard the voice of the Lord tell me clearly that my name for the rest of the earth-journey is Raven. Oh if you could have seen my face, one eyebrow up and head cocked. "Tell me more." This was the only response I could evoke. I heard that "Every raven story is your story and part of your divine design."

I heard that I was like the frustrated, sneaky raven in the tale told by the Tlingit indigenous peoples of the Pacific Northwest Coast of North America, *How Raven Stole the Sun*. I was encouraged to "steal the sun and return light to the world" through my work. Responses from my students and clients would reflect back to me that, indeed, they had more light in their world after spending time in our practices. I was honored to be their guide during pivotal parts of their journey.

More raven stories would pass through my mind as I lingered in *The Center*. The raven story in the Old Testament of The Bible, for example, in which ravens fed the prophet Elijah under direct instruction from God each morning.

Raven stories continue to pour into my awareness, and I resonate with each one in a special way. My love for birds that had been present in my youth has come full circle.

RETURN JOURNEY

I see stars above the red rocks of southern Utah each night that I'm in my home. There is minimal light pollution where I am. Ravens fly past me daily now, and when they perch, we talk, laugh, and plan. We talk about the turmoil of the world. We know *The Center* is still present. Daily, I have the opportunity and the gift of living out my personal Sacred Redesign. It's become more of a process than a destination. It is the daily act of walking it out, as it unfolds. Being in the midst of it is amazing.

My Sacred Redesign has become a way of life now. I greet each day with wonder and inquiry. "What is mine to do today?" My best-laid plans often are enhanced and sacredly redesigned in the moment. Always proving beneficial to me and those I'm around. I love being a part of the design process.

One of my favorite morning practices is to sit with fresh hot coffee, a mixed media pad of paper, strongly pigmented markers, water-soluble crayons from Switzerland, a small paintbrush, and a bit of water. I take a sip and allow my intuition to begin to receive the energy of the day. I witness the energy unfold on the paper as my hand applies ink and color. I intuitively reach for the colors that request to be a part of the day's design. I sense what is being required from me. I sense what gifts there are to open, and even activate. It is a form of prayer, blended with the deep listening of meditation, and planning with pigments.

I use my formal day planner as a way to track commitments and appointments, and my daily drawing as a way to weave in the current energy and instructions from *The Center*. I intentionally have spaciousness planned on the front end of my day in order to ease into the day. It supports my heart and soul. It keeps me sure-footed, as the topsy-turvy world spins on. I stay tethered to *The Center* world.

The daily walk of my life is now my living art. It is the expression of the intuitive, internal images out-pictured. It is the substrate—I am the medium. One could say that this "return journey" from "center" in my labyrinth walk is like walking between worlds. I have the direct daily experience of being on the path with its winding curves. I am in the midst of the tribulation of this world and simultaneously in the midst of the peace of *The Center* world. I am not fully in one or the other, rather intentionally striding in both. It is a wonderful place to be.

My hope is that you can find your place as you walk out your labyrinth, as well as the ease of the stride between worlds. Perhaps our paths will intersect in the near future. Until then, I wish you peace and even a return of your own playfulness.

ABOUT THE AUTHOR

Jolynn Van Asten AKA Raven is the founder of The Raven Art Institute™ and The Raven Art Experience™.

She is a sought-after trainer of Brain-Based Leadership and Intuitive Expressive Art.

She is the co-author of *Uncensored. Untamed. Unleashed.: How Soulful Entrepreneurs Are Leading into the Golden Age*, co-author and illustrator of the *I Am a Difference Maker* children's creativity book, and the author of the forthcoming children's book, *The Dream Of The Little Buffalo*, which tells the tale of how creativity can eradicate the effects of human suffering.

She runs certification programs in the Raven Art Institute method of intuitive expressive arts, virtual and in-person well-being retreats, and works privately with clients who seek transformation and greater well-being via customized intuitive expressive art experiences.

Website: www.ravenartinstitute.com
Email: info@ravenartinstitute.com

21

DR. KRISTINA TICKLER WELSOME

OUR SACRED SELF

ndividually designed in the image of the Creator, we may find ourselves similar to others in certain ways, yet we are uniquely sacred members of the human race. How sacred do you hold your image of the Divine? Do you honor the divine within your Self? Your body is a sacred vessel. It is the home of your heart, mind, soul, and the keeper of the life force that is your breath. Do you treat it like the sacred container that it is?

"The body is your temple. Keep it pure and clean for the soul to reside in."
- B.K.S. Iyengar

During your lifetime, perhaps you or others have desecrated this holiest of temples. Instead of treading on hallowed ground, you were trampled. Instead of being blessed, venerated and revered, you were cursed, unprotected, and disrespected. Perhaps you self-abandoned instead of providing yourself with the reverence and respect you are entitled to. Please know that as a child of God, you were born inherently worthy. There is nothing you need to do to earn or sustain that worth. It is your birthright.

This sacred belief is one that I hold to be unquestionably true. It is deeply ingrained in me, yet I wasn't aware I even held it. Spirituality is the last one of my 8 Keys to Wellness I held, which when finally inserted allowed me to unlock and learn to love my authentic Self. For too long I confused my religious upbringing with the spiritual relationship I longed for in my life.

"Religion is belief in someone else's experience. Spirituality is having your own experience." - Deepak Chopra

The truth of the matter is that spirituality is perhaps the most natural thing there is. For me, it is simply my own conscious Self recognizing that I am more than just a body, that I am a soul with infinite potential. Spirituality allows me to be more fully present in each moment of my life. To have a truly lived experience, flourishing and finding hope amidst pain and difficulties. To find meaning and purpose in the things that I value. It allows me to search for inner freedom, well-being, and peace of mind. To show up as love in relationship with myself and others, with a sense of belonging and connection to the universe. In my spirituality, I have a connection with myself and all of life on a soul level.

To me, God isn't an external construct that I seek to please or fear for retribution. God is usually considered to possess the following essential attributes: Omnipotent (limitless power), Omniscient (limitless knowledge), Eternal (limitless time), Good (limitless benevolence), and Unified (unable to be divided). If God exists within all of us, then the Divine can be defined as a universal and fundamental source of all physical existence. We each hold within us the possibility of the power, knowledge, and benevolence to unify all of humanity for eternity.

Once I recognized that God existed within me and for me, I was able to work towards compassion, forgiveness, and self-love. I learned to show respect for myself as a sacred being in the ways that I thought and felt, how I spoke, how I acted, and how I cared for myself and others. My body is a temple, and I am a goddess. I now treat myself with the honor that I deserve. This perspective shift has allowed me to see myself more clearly, as I redesign my sacred self. People who are hurt, hurt other people--but healing people can heal the world.

"No matter who you are, no matter what you did, no matter where you've come from, you can always change, become a better version of yourself." – Madonna

Like redoing our home, so too can our sacred heart, mind, soul, and body undergo redesign. We declutter the unnecessary junk. We reorganize and put things where they belong so we can see them more clearly. We shed the inauthentic layers that were put on us by others. We may need to break down some walls to open things up to flow better. We redesign the space and the internal landscape to reflect the sacred being we are. We decorate it to celebrate our dedication and hard work and to highlight our uniqueness. Once we have returned to our own true nature, we can host an open house to welcome those who have shared in our expansion.

Even as we welcome others into our most sacred space, we must continue to honor and be responsible for caring for the most important person in our own life: our Self. In most ways, you are the only one who can take care of yourself. Buddhist teachers are quick to point out that while we are admonished to have compassion and love for all beings, we must not forget to extend that all important compassion to ourselves! We can not take care of others or our tasks to our fullest capacity, with mindfulness, grace, and passion, if we are not taking time to care for ourselves. There are countless practices we can engage in to help recharge and nurture our beings, such as meditation, breathwork, yoga, exercise, spending time in nature, and creativity. Choose to engage with them regularly to fill your well of being with more vibrance and light. Our being needs periods of solitude, space, and silence to process the world, speak to us, and guide us into co-creation with the Universe.

When we feel safe and in integrity with who we truly are, we can embrace this divine nature in ourselves and others, and more easily bridge the divide of "us versus them," joining together as the "we" the world so desperately needs. The Indian greeting of Namaste translates to "the divine in me sees the divine in you". This serves in acknowledgment that we are all interconnected, that no one person is more important than any other, and that we actively respect this each and every time we greet somebody. I think this principle of seeing ourselves in others is crucial for human society to move forward with grace. It is important for us to remember to respect and to revere our Self, our fellow human beings, and all of the creatures of our precious earth.

Come home to the sacred Self that lives within you. This is your heaven on earth.

ABOUT THE AUTHOR

Dr. Tina Tickler Welsome is a doctor of Physical Therapy, owner of The Key To Wellness and The Key Publishing, a Holistic Life Transformation coach, and international bestselling author and publisher. Decades of professional experience with patients, students, and clients makes her coaching effective, efficient, and easily integrated into your life. Her passion is to support the well-being and healing of your heart, mind, body, and soul as you learn to love your authentic self. Tina will empower you to become the author of your own life story as you discover unconsidered possibilities, remove barriers to success and unlock your full potential to live a creative life you love. Her own life journey prepared her to use her voice to amplify the voices of others to create even more impact in the world. You can find her living her best life as a mom of three divine masculine men in the making and expanding her own potential as a perfectly imperfect human being.

Website: www.thekeytowellness.net
Facebook: www.facebook.com/kristina.welsome
and www.facebook.com/thekeytowellness.net
and www.facebook.com/groups/soulnourishingconversations
Twitter: www.twitter.com/drtinawelsome
Instagram: www.instagram.com/thekeytowellness.tina
LinkedIn: www.linkedin.com/in/drkristinawelsome
Email: tina@thekeytowellness.net

22

MICHALL J MEDINA

FROM ROCK BOTTOM TO FREEDOM: HOW I FREED MYSELF FROM ANXIETY & CLAIMED MY TRUE CALLING

THE ROCK BOTTOM

It was a cloudy summer day as I looked up at the sky, begging and pleading for a miracle. I had hit rock bottom, and I had no fight left in me. I begged for something to happen to save me from this dark misery that had become my life. As I sobbed uncontrollably, it was the deepest pain I had ever felt. I knew that something needed to change, but I had no clue how I would pull myself out of this despair.

This is what had become of my life after a sudden onset of social anxiety. Before this had happened, I was going out with friends, making new friends, and I was the life of the party. I loved my life and loved spreading positivity and joy everywhere I went. Until one day, a group of friends rejected me. Unbeknownst to me, I had an extremely fragile sense of self-worth and had built my entire life on receiving love and validation from others. I was outgoing and friendly because I needed others to like me and approve of me. Until one day, no matter how hard I tried, I couldn't get this group of friends to change their minds about me. It felt like they hated me and there was nothing I could do about it, and it was that realization that brought my world crumbling down to the ground.

At this time, I was working as an electrical engineer, and my job allowed the flexibility of working from home if I'd choose to. So, mostly, if not every day, during this time, I'd stay at home. When the social anxiety first started, I could still go to the office and feel fine. It seemed that the anxiety was directly related to me feeling like I needed to show my true self, and at work, I felt like I could just play the professional role and hide my true self. Eventually though, as more and more fears started to creep in, I started to be afraid of even going to work out of fear that the anxiety might get triggered.

Suddenly, I found myself feeling unsafe everywhere I went because I could run into someone I knew at any moment and then the anxiety would get triggered. This eventually led to me being afraid to even leave my house.

In this perspective of doom and gloom that had become my life, it felt like my entire world was turning against me. It felt like my friends weren't there for me, the religious community I was living in at the time judged me and criticized me, and I knew that engineering wasn't what I wanted to do with the rest of my life.

I felt stuck and hopeless. I wanted to end my life, but I knew that if I did, my parents would be devastated. It was at this rock bottom that I decided that the only option was to find a solution.

THE GLIMMER OF HOPE & THE SEARCH FOR A SOLUTION

As I spoke to my sister on the phone, opening up to her about the anxiety and depression, a glimmer of hope set in when she told me about cognitive behavioral therapy and anti-depressants.

"Finally, a way out of this misery!" I thought to myself—"a way to fix whatever went wrong in my brain that started triggering this anxiety."

So, I set up an appointment with my doctor and convinced her to prescribe me anti-depressants and refer me to a cognitive behavioral therapist.

At the cognitive behavioral therapist's office, she explained to me various techniques I could use to manage the anxiety whenever it would come up.

"So, I'm going to have to live with this anxiety for the rest of my life?" I thought to myself. I became determined to find another solution, because somehow, I knew that if this anxiety had been triggered suddenly, then there must be some way to undo whatever happened in my brain so I can get back to how I was before—happy, free, and confident around people.

So, my search for a solution continued. I went to see a trauma therapist next. In my session with her, she asked me many questions around what happened with the group of friends. She explained that by revisiting and talking about the experience, I can come to a resolution of the traumatic experience. "There has to be a better way to get to the core root of whatever this is," I thought to myself. So, I continued my search.

Next, I went to see a hypnotherapist. He guided me through a deep relaxation where he would tell me that I am confident. To my surprise, after my session with him, I had regained my confidence and ability to be myself around people! But as the days went on, the anxiety would come back. I went to a couple more sessions with him and quickly realized that if I wanted the anxiety to go away permanently and completely, I would have to keep going to hypnotherapy sessions for the rest of my life. "There has to be a better way," I thought to myself. So, my search continued.

Eventually, I started to explore alternative forms of therapy, including EMDR, EFT Tapping, energy healing, ThetaHealing®, Energy Medicine, Reiki, QHHT®, One Brain®, RTT®, psychic readings and healings, Akashic Records readings and clearings, and Ayahuasca ceremonies and retreats. Any type of healing modality you can think of, I probably tried it.

As I went through this healing and discovery journey over the course of several years, I got better at managing the anxiety. There started being fewer and fewer times that the anxiety would get triggered. I felt free for the most part except for the few times that the anxiety would still get triggered.

Though I had found some relief and started feeling more and more like myself, I continued the search for a solution because I was determined to reach a point where the anxiety would never get triggered again. I was determined to be and feel 100% free.

It was this level of determination that led me to finding the true solution.

FINDING THE TRUE SOLUTION

Throughout my journey of learning, exploring, and healing, I realized how I was blocking myself from being able to heal completely.

I realized that this entire time I had been seeing the anxiety as something bad—something that needed to be fixed. It was one of my mentors who helped me see that the anxiety was just a manifestation of an aspect of myself that was hurt and trying to protect itself. So, by rejecting that part of myself and treating it as my enemy, I was only perpetuating the endless cycle of constantly needing to find "healing" from it.

By rejecting that part of me by wanting the anxiety to be gone, I wasn't allowing that part of me to be integrated back into wholeness and love. I quickly realized that by shifting my mindset around the anxiety, I was opening a pathway for the anxiety to truly shift.

THE SHIFT

The anxiety didn't resolve immediately though. What followed was a transformation of myself as the one seeking healing to the one serving others and guiding them on their paths of transformation.

Back when I was working in engineering, I knew that this wasn't the path for me. Deep down, I knew that my passion was to help others, but back then, I had no clue how I would do this.

Fast forward two years, and now I had all of this knowledge, training and experience in almost every healing modality invented. And on top of that, I had directly experienced the power of shifting my mindset around my experiences and how that makes all the difference between constantly seeking healing to being able to truly shift and integrate back into wholeness.

So, when it came time to start searching for another job, I thought to myself "What am I doing?! Isn't this why I quit my engineering job in the first place? To find what I'm truly passionate about!" So, I decided that now was the time to start helping others. I enrolled in a life coaching certification course, and so began my journey of building my own business and serving others.

My business didn't take off immediately though. What followed was nearly a year and a half of me trying things and getting nowhere. It wasn't until I took a step back and resolved all of the fears, self-doubts and insecurities that I had around showing up in the world as a leader that my business really started to gain traction. It was this shift within myself that created space for the clarity, intuitions, and inspirations to come in that would lead me towards creating the programs and services that were truly aligned to my heart's true calling—the unique perspectives that only I have and the unique gifts that I have to offer.

Eventually, I no longer had to worry about the anxiety because I was on a much greater path. My life had purpose and meaning, and as I continued to grow and evolve alongside my business, my mind's focus completely left behind the story of overcoming anxiety.

THE CLARITY

Looking back now, I see it so clearly. How could I have ever permanently and completely shifted the anxiety while I was replaying the story of needing to "overcome anxiety." I was keeping myself small and not allowing myself to evolve into the next level version of me. But once I gave myself permission to claim my true calling and started making progress every day towards that direction, even if it wasn't clear at first, I started to grow and evolve into a new person. It's like the intention of stepping into my true calling in and of itself catalyzed the growth that needed to happen within me to take me to a new version of myself. And by setting that intention for myself, the shedding of old limitations and identities came more easily. Gone were the days of struggling with something for days, weeks, months or even years. I started to be able to shift and resolve whatever triggers came up with little to no struggle and very quickly. I realized that all the struggle that I had experienced in the past was entirely due to my own resistance. My resistance to change, and my resistance to evolving into a new version of me.

Now I'm so clear on my passion of helping aspiring heart-centered visionaries to claim their true calling without waiting to feel ready. By sharing the mindset strategies and methods that I developed to shift out of my old patterns effortlessly, I help each one of them to become a new person, and by doing so, they become a magnet to new opportunities to come their way, paving the path forward towards their vision of claiming their true calling. It's no longer a struggle, there's no more confusion and lack of clarity. They tune into a higher path of ease and flow, and in turn, they reconnect to their passion, love and joy.

I strongly believe that had I not started following my true passion of helping others, I never would have been able to find the joy, freedom and fulfillment that I now have in my life.

THE CALL

One thing I learned in this whole process is that when your heart is calling you forth, the longer you postpone answering that call, the more pain and discomfort you create for yourself. When you experience pain and struggle in your life, it is only a symptom of resistance, and by resisting the process, you only create more struggle. You don't need healing; you just need to move in the direction of your passion and live your life the way you want to. Because when you do, you'll start to see everything rearrange itself for you to allow you to continue on the path you've set out to achieve. You don't need to know exactly how everything will play out. All you need to do is shift your intention towards living the life you want to live and cultivate a willingness, desire, and determination to start living that way now. Because when you do, you set in motion for all the layers of unworthiness, fears and insecurities to come to surface so that they can be shifted, so that you can reintegrate those parts of yourself back into wholeness. And as you continually evolve into a new person, you leave the struggles and worries behind and tap into a flow of inspiration that carries you forward without the struggle and hard work. Life starts happening for you, and the path forward reveals itself as you continue on this path. Every part of your life starts to shift. Your health improves because you're fueled by the energy of living your passion. Your relationships improve because you're more deeply connected with your heart and feel safe enough to take down those walls. You no longer live in a scarcity mindset, and the doors of opportunity fly open for you. You realize that you can have anything you want, and you begin to create your reality consciously and deliberately.

Now looking back, I realize that the goal was never really to get back to how I was before the anxiety started, because in truth, even though I was confident around people, my confidence was built around a foundation of seeking validation and receiving my self-worth from others. Now that I've grown and evolved into this new version of me, I gain my sense of self-worth from within. No longer do I need to reaffirm my self-worth through others. My whole life is now built on a foundation of self-love, and that is the greatest freedom I could have ever asked for.

ABOUT THE AUTHOR

Michall J Medina is an award-winning spiritual and mindset coach and an international bestselling author and speaker. She helps aspiring heart-centered visionaries to claim their true calling without waiting to feel ready, by amplifying their ability to intuitively attract opportunity. Before she launched her business, Michall had trained in over seven different healing modalities in search for a cure for her anxiety. As a former electrical engineer, she brought her analytical skills to the world of healing and spirituality and developed a ground-breaking method of resolving the core root of any struggle and shifting it into expansion and freedom. She now shares this method with her clients all over the world. Michall has been featured for her work in Yahoo Finance, Fox News, International Business Times, Wall Street Select, and Digital Journal. Originally a Texan, she now lives in Israel by the forest with her beautiful cat Stella.

Website: www.michalljmedina.com
Facebook: www.facebook.com/michalljmedina
Email: michall@michalljmedina.com

23

SABRINA RUNBECK

IS YOUR NETWORK TRULY YOUR NET WORTH?

How much do you value your connections with others? Brene Brown said, "Connection is why we're here; it is what gives purpose and meaning to our lives."

May I ask you: How are you connecting with the key players in your network? Add the digital era into the mix, things become tough when we are transforming our team to a work-from-home setup, conversing with clients virtually, and even seeing our clinicians via telemedicine apps.

Building meaningful connections is hard enough in person now that we have added challenges from the virtual world. What if you could have the right tools to consistently attract the right talents? More importantly, what if you could choose to retain only the A-players in your inner circle and let go of the less qualified ones that spoil your team?

It would be a game changer!

Networking is vital for everyone who wants to move up in their career. A survey found that 85% of jobs are filled through networking. This is vital for those mid level managers who want to move up the ladder or the brave souls who are starting their own business.

Allow me to share a quick story. Eight years ago, I had four job offers even before I got my medical license. How did I do it? Through networking.

At the time, I looked up career events from each hospital I wanted to be part of and made sure to show up with a few resumes at hand. For example, there was this one event hosted by Meridian Healthcare system in Jersey City. I drove from Philadelphia, where I was living at the time, to Jersey City just to make an appearance without expectations. Then, I headed directly to those who are running the event to introduce myself. There was no better way than showing the recruiters who you are in person.

After building a brief rapport, I asked to be connected to the person who was helping to hire positions that I was applying for. Guess what? She had four positions that I didn't even know existed. She then asked me which ones I wanted to consider for interviews!

Networking is also a must for maintaining your business. Executives reviewed that they would lose 28% of their business if they stopped networking. It is a part of their daily activities for business growth. I intentionally block off time to engage with people who are my potential clients and collaborators daily for 15 minutes. This is how I grew my clientele for my practice—by leveraging other people's networks to create win-win situations for everyone.

The primary thing about creating win-win situations is sharing resources, which makes a fertile ground for friendship. Zig Ziglar said, "You can have everything in life if you just help enough people get what they want". Your network is your net worth and it is a social investment. Like any type of investment, it requires the right attention and effort. When done right and with the right strategy, you become the magnet of talent.

Through my journey of building mental fitness and self-mastery, I learned five essential concepts to create irresistible influence and impact by collaboration. Before we dive in, let me introduce myself. I am Sabrina Runbeck, MPH, MHS, PA-C. I am a Cardiothoracic Surgery Physician Associate and an expert in public health and neuroscience with more than 10 years of experience.

The Association of American Medical College found there will be a significant shortage of physicians (122,000) in the U.S. by 2032. This drop is due to long work hours, burnout, and a reduction of revenue. Can you imagine what would happen to your family when providers leave their practices? Who would be left to take care of us and put us in the center of their care?

After overcoming burnout, I became an International Peak Performance Keynote Speaker and Advisor. Now I empower ambitious and overwhelmed healthcare private practice owners and their team to gain a day a week. When they know how to create efficiency by gaining self-mastery and create a fail-proof environment, then they can exponentially increase their profit while improving patient satisfaction.

After implementing my six-core system of the Provider's Edge program, my clients stop having endless to-do lists, constantly putting out fires, and then became able to move steadily forward. I believe with the right strategies, every healthcare leader can minimize their time to create maximum outcomes. They can have a double win in both work and life.

That's why people call me the Queen of Performance and Productivity.

Are you ready to become irresistible to others? Let's dive into our first strategy.

STRATEGY #1: BE A THOUGHT LEADER

A Thought Leader is someone who, based on their expertise and perspective in an industry, offers unique guidance, inspires innovation and influences others.

A Thought Leader has three qualities:

First, they teach us how to think so we can discover beyond the norm. They ignite their team to think differently compared with the traditional ways things have been done.

Secondly, Thought Leaders are similar to coaches who challenge us to be better. They can't just demand every single play to happen even if they have a plan, but they help their colleagues to face obstacles. They challenge their team members to do slightly better than their status quo.

Lastly, Thought Leaders serve as role models. You may think that people don't notice you, but in reality, people subconsciously pick up everything that you do. We have learned from neuroscience a group of cells called Mirror Neurons. It's similar to kids copying every move or people adapting to accents from a new region. People will notice how you show up on a daily basis.

STRATEGY #2: BE AN INSTANT CONNECTOR

Picture this, when you start a conversation, people are drawn to you. How powerful would this be when you want to have more clients, better earning, and a finer lifestyle? Ask yourself how you can become that magnetized and not feel awkward when everyone else is talking.

The answer: learn how to listen.

You might be hearing what people are telling you but are you truly listening effectively? There are two types of effective listening: Active Listening and Strategic Listening.

We will use the acronym HEAR to explain Active Listening.

H stands for Halt.

This means that you want to stop what you're doing and give people your full attention. There is a phenomenon that creates distrust and disrespect in the current era. This behavior is called "Fobbing", and we want to avoid this. Fobbing means that you can't have a conversation with people without checking your phones for alerts, text messages, and emails. How can you truly listen if you are being distracted and pulled into different directions?

E stands for Empathy.

People want to be understood because they are looking for empathy. What are they telling you? Can you connect with them with similar stories? Empathy is also one of the five Sage powers in Positive Intelligence. Part of our mental power that can be trained.

A stands for Anticipate.

Where does this conversation lead? What do they really want to share next? Take an adventure with your counterpart. When your minds are synchronized, you can finish each other's sentences.

R stands for Review.

You have to paraphrase in a way that people will feel like you understood them. Formulate as a question or statement to make sure you heard them correctly. It doesn't mean that you have to repeat everything.

Strategic Listening, on the other hand, is a little step further where listening becomes an activity where you are involved with their story. You try to understand them while enjoying the conversation to get something out of them. You listen with such awareness to know what they want to emphasize.

You also need to change your tonality and phrasing so you can mimic them. It is similar to conversing with your friend by matching each other's pace and emotional state. Lastly, you want to listen and find out other people's desires; what they truly want to solve and create.

STRATEGY #3: BE A QUESTION MASTER

Let's dive a little deeper to truly discover what your counterpart wants. Be wary of how you ask questions because people may interpret your motives differently. Instead of acknowledging that you want to hear more, they may think that you are questioning their ideas. This is mostly evident to new people that you meet in an interview session, peer discussion, or new hires joining your team.

Recently, I worked with a neurosensory doctor. She opened up about the problem that one of her therapists was slacking off. The first time she brought this up to me, I asked her, "Did you have a conversation with her to address these concerns?" She was wary of becoming confrontational. She wants to keep her employees happy. I challenged her and asked if it was really a confrontation or simply a difficult conversation? We have to make a mindset shift from a judger to a learner. This is where the power of questioning comes into place because it allows you to learn more about the situation.

Here are the differences between these two paths. One, you can take the learner's path where you wish to know what the problem is and what solution you can give. You can even ask for their proposals and how they can solve their own problems.

On the other hand, you may lean toward a judger's path, which is not a good thing. A judge's line of questioning seeks to determine who is at fault and focuses on the causes of the problems. In term, this reflects negatively on you. We want to be in the former where the questions focus on understanding the situation and solving the problem in future tense.

STRATEGY #4: BE A BOUNDARY SETTER

You can also grow your network by being a stickler about your boundaries. I believe that if your circle of friends are not inspiring you, then you don't have a circle. Rather, you have a mental cage.

There is a story about a white tiger that was gifted to the National Zoo in Washington DC. Initially, the zoo did not have the capability to host this tiger, Mohini. Therefore, he was caged inside a 12x12 metal box while the zookeepers built a giant park for him. The tiger paced around at the outskirts of the box day after day. When the zoo finally finished the park with rocks, trees, little hills, they released Mohini to his new home. Guess what? He found a corner of his new home and started pacing a 12x12 square path, like he had done in his cage before.

Do we really need to keep ourselves enclosed for what we used to know, instead of being able to expand with the right people? There are energy vampires out there, and it's okay to let them go. Not all great people are meant to fit in with all cultures. We all have limited attention spans. We should not let other people suck away our precious time, energy and most importantly, our sanity.

A concept called sensationalism states that our mind is focused on where our direction goes. For example, whenever we say we're too busy, it becomes a weakness. Being busy means you cannot truly focus on what's most important. It can feel that we're productive, but in reality, it is not efficient. It is just doing more work.

We have to figure out what our mental diet is. I would suggest doing this quick exercise right now. Put a bookmark on this page, then grab a pen and paper. Write down where you are getting all your information on a daily basis. It can be a social media platform, newspaper, news alerts, or community message boards. Next, write down how much time you are spending on each of them every day.

This exercise should give you some overview of how you spend your time. Some of you may not realize it until you switch to a different activity before noticing that you haven't eaten, picked up the laundry, or done something more valuable. We can remedy this mindset by performing a mental diet and cleansing.

Beyond doing a clean up of your own bad habits, let's further examine the people that are composed in your immediate environment. For the next exercise, think about all the key components, like the people in your life and your team members. Do they weigh you down like anchors or do they drive you forward like an engine? Try to categorize each person where they belong. It is also crucial to select and recognize which organizations you should retain or dissolve. We want to be in groups where people are wiser and more successful than us. At a minimum, they are at the same level of our drive, so we can lead us to a better state. Now you have a more systematic way to evaluate who you have to set boundaries around.

We have to find the right people who want to build a collaborative relationship to go forward together, such as a power partner. Once they are found, we have to create an environment where they want to stay. These are the people you share your time, energy, and knowledge with. Therefore, you can also tap into each other's networks for resources to boost your effectiveness and value.

The theory of Dunbar's number says that we can only maintain about 150 relationships at any given time. Tapping into this human tendency, the 5-50-100 rule was created by Judy Robinett, author of *How to be a Power Connector*. The first five people are those you are most connected to and trusted. They can be friends, family, mentors, and partners from work. The next fifty people are within your inner circle. They are those who, when asked, will help you or your friends in need. You can call them and send them an email and they'll get back to you within 24 hours with a solution. As for the next 100, these are people that come and go, they watch you from a distance and are willing to support you when they are available.

How do you strengthen your 150 relationships? The essential five are the people who you get in touch with on a daily if not weekly basis. Your inner circle fifty are those people that you probably keep in touch with on a weekly basis, if not bi-weekly. And then the top 100 at least once a month. You may share an interesting moment of your life or an opportunity they might benefit from.

Jim Rohn said, "You are the average of the five people you spend the most time with." Let's figure out how you are being influenced by these five essential influencers in your life. For the next exercise, you would rate these five people's attributes based on your knowledge of them.

Then, you ask each of them to rate themselves based on following attributes from one to ten, with ten being the highest:

1. Physical health
2. Mental well-being
3. Professional career
4. Financial intelligence
5. Spirituality
6. Romantic relationships
7. Family situation
8. Social support
9. Personal growth
10. Overall lifestyle

Perform a self-assessment as well. Then, tally your scores and compare each attribute side-by-side. Where are they different? Are they really aligned with where you need to be and want to be? You can also write down the top three qualities of the people that truly inspire and motivate you to move forward.

Everything is interconnected. It is vital for you to choose the right people who can help you to constantly move forward. Whether it is leading your own business or moving up within an organization. You don't have to do it alone.

Find a partner out there—a fellow peak performer—who can keep you accountable. This person is someone I will encourage you to have regular meetings with. Think about how you help and challenge each other to be better? In order to do this successfully, this person must have a complimentary personality. At the end of the day, we just need to be a little bit better each day.

So let me ask you, we talked about five concepts: Be a thought leader, an Instant Connector, a Question Master, a Boundary Setter, and a Power Partner. Which one would you like to tap into today? Which one do you want to focus on first? All five are important, which means that you probably have some of these in the back of your pocket. Leverage those attributes you do well, and then pick one to implement and get you to the next level.

Today, I host the Provider's Edge podcast where I meet amazing healthcare leaders to share their stories of struggle and triumph in order to inspire others to develop an edge to scale their practices and themselves. I am an international bestselling author of the book, *Asian Women Who BossUp*. I also spoke on numerous stages such as FOX, CBS, ABC, KevinMD, and Live on Purpose Radio. While empowering other healthcare leaders to have a double win in both work and life, I am still practicing in surgery.

These career highlights didn't come over a day. They were built by leveraging relationship economics persistently. You can do it, too. Let's begin by connecting with each other. Take out your phone, go to LinkedIn, and connect with me.

My profile url is *www.Linkedin.com/in/SabrinaRunbeck.*

Starting from this moment forward, you can compound other people's talent, network, and time to accelerate your mission with the least amount of resources.

ABOUT THE AUTHOR

After overcoming burnout working in cardiothoracic surgery, Sabrina Runbeck, MPH, MHS, PA-C became a keynote speaker and advisor supporting healthcare practice owners and their teams to gain back a day a week.

She believes with the right systems, every healthcare leader can create the ultimate time makeover where they can spend less time, earn higher profit, and enjoy life more.

Therefore, Sabrina integrated her background in medicine, neuroscience, and positive intelligence to guide her clients to stop having endless to-do lists or constantly putting out fires, and be able to move forward consistently.

That's why people call her the Queen of Performance and Productivity.

She hosts the Provider's Edge Podcast and is an international bestselling author being featured on Thrive Global, Authority Magazine, Fox, CBS, and ABC.

Website: www.SabrinaRunbeck.com

24

SHAYNA MELISSA STOCKMAN

SACRED HEART: SHAYNA MELISSA FOLLOWED HER SACRED HEART

My grandmother grew up poor, Jewish, with divorced parents, during the prior pandemic and great depression, to graduate high school two years early. I was raised by this grandmother and also grew up poor, Jewish, from divorced parents, but in a rich, Catholic, two-parent household kind of community. To overcome what we were born into, we had to overachieve. I emulated my grandmother to become a very shy, sweet, polite and respectful young lady. We both enjoyed helping others and putting smiles on everyone's faces.

As a little girl, I would witness Grandma swallow her pill (a potassium-depleting diuretic for her blood pressure) with a banana and order foods without salt. Years later, in health classes, I would realize the power of foods for medicinal purposes (bananas contain potassium), as well as the ill consequences of foods (i.e., salty foods retain water that raises blood pressure and too much sugar intake may contribute to diabetes). Grandma's siblings all ate poorly and developed diabetes while she ate healthy, stayed slender, and never developed diabetes. Since my entire upbringing in the 1970s, I had been studying this more natural approach from both Grandma and what Grandpa—the pharmacist—had taught her. (In later years, I confirmed my suspicion that we have the power to actually change genetic expression i.e., the family tendency to develop diabetes.)

One day, a very sweet and special nurse left a lasting impression on me.

I thought 'OMG! She will never know how many lives she has impacted, and how many of those lives will, in turn, impact more lives.' That was my "aha" moment; I thought, 'Nurses like to help people. I like to help people. Like her, I want to impact many lives that, in turn, impact many more lives! My passion to help others will create, not a mere rippling effect, but a massive tidal wave of people helping people, each putting smiles on even more faces.' This has led me toward a life-long career in nursing. Learning from Grandma, I wanted to emphasize a more natural approach that actually attacks the root cause.

Eventually, doctors left my grandma with no good treatment plan to ever walk again. She looked up to me, the new nurse, and asked, "Do you think I will ever walk again?" I was not used to this role reversal. I knew to get her walking again, I needed to find and attack the root cause. Also, our thoughts control our actions that dictate our results. So, I gave her the belief that she would walk again and said, "Yes! You will walk again!" With belief, a vision, consistent daily action (stretching and strengthening exercises), and perseverance, she walked again, without assistance, a walker or even a cane!

By age 26, I earned five college degrees, four nursing licenses, two Nurse Practitioner (NP) licenses, a National Board Certification and a perfect 4.0 GPA with my post master's degree. I've now been an RN (Registered Nurse) for over 30 years and a Nationally Board-Certified NP who is dual-licensed as both an Adult and Child Health NP for three decades.

A few years later, my vital organ, my Sacred Heart, was failing; the specialists left me feeling abandoned, helpless and hopeless. But I had belief that I could overcome this, attacked the root cause, and helped *heal myself holistically without medications.*

I went from heart failure and failing English to helping heal myself without medications and writing about it to become a #1 International Best-Selling Author of Overcoming Life Obstacles (OLO)!

OLO goes into more depth about a proactive approach, prevention, overcoming heart failure, reversing dis-order, activating your genes, as well as how to Biohack your Body Back to Better health to re-energize, feel better and be happier.

As a Nationally Board-Certified NP for 3 decades, I have *healed thousands holistically*. My passion is to help millions more who were also left hopeless by their doctors to overcome, re-energize, feel better, and be happier, often without medications. By empowering my fellow healthcare professionals with my same techniques and *simple* solutions internationally, I've created, not a mere rippling effect, but that massive tidal wave effect.

My heart!!! My SACRED HEART-

Listen to your intuition and follow your sacred heart. Over 46,000 EXTRA heartbeats in 24 hours threw my heart into heart failure. My vital organ was failing! The heart doctor wanted me to ignore my symptoms. Do not ignore your body's warning signs. If your healthcare providers are not getting you healthy, consider firing them! That's exactly what I did. I had to believe that I could come out of heart failure. "Where there is a will there's a way." I can NOT fail if I do not quit. Quitting was not an option with my LIFE!

When I can attack the root cause, I can stop progression, often reverse dis-order, rid symptoms and decrease the need for pharmaceutical dependencies (medications).

For example, my patient's obesity caused his high blood pressure, diabetes and knee pain. After I helped him lose over 100 pounds, his high blood pressure, diabetes and knee pain resolved without medications.

So, for myself, I had to do the same—*find the cause to find the solution.* You can read more about how I helped heal myself holistically without medications in my book *Overcoming Life Obstacles*. OLO went on to become a #1 International Bestseller in multiple countries and categories.

Subtle differences in health care roles and what I CHOOSE:

RNs cannot prescribe. So I decided to advance my education and licenses to order the correct tests, treatments and medications that my patients deserved. Since physician assistants generally work under physicians' supervision and NPs may work independently of physicians, I chose to become an NP. Wanting to treat people of all ages, led me to earn both adult and child health NP licenses.

As an NP, I perform similar duties to those of a doctor: I obtain the patients' histories (allergies, medications...), render thorough physical examinations, order, and interpret laboratory and diagnostic tests. I also diagnose, educate to empower, offer natural, healthy alternative options, and prescribe medications when needed. Procedures I perform include: starting IVs, blood draws, joint aspirations, incisions, drains, foreign body removals, biopsies, casting, suturing, stapling, and insertion of catheters and airways.

I thought: there are cancer centers everywhere, but how many preventive centers have you seen? I'd rather warn a child to wear a helmet than treat his head injury.

I'd rather be *ProActive* to *prevent* your dis-order *today* than

ReActive to *treat* your dis-order *tomorrow*!

Modern medicine often tries to fix the problem *after* the fact. Once the damage is done, it's often irreversible, what I call the "hard-boiled egg syndrome." I'd rather *prevent* a heart attack than try to reverse the permanent/irreversible damage (dead heart muscle).

Rather than most practitioners who only use western (synthetic) *or* eastern medicine (more natural alternatives), I use what is best for that individual patient and unique situation. It may be a natural alternative, a medication, or both. For decades, before there was even a school for functional (root cause) medicine, I have been merging eastern alternatives with western medicine (aka "integrative medicine") to attack the root cause, produce synergistic effects and better outcomes.

Some problems may be avoided, controlled, or even reverted with a combination of proper nutrition, weight reduction, physical fitness, life-style changes (i.e., smoke cessation) and other Biohacking methods that I call *"not just supplementation, but ACTIVATION."* Activation is actually activating, or stimulating, *vital* pathways in our body to do what they used to do and should do, to work more efficiently.

Biohacking means to hack, or try to take control over, your own biology. We can *Biohack with nutrients that affect our genes/genetic expression.* For example, when Grandma ate well and stayed slender, she avoided her family's tendency of diabetes from being genetically expressed. Biohacking seems to be more than just "masking tape on a garden hose." It seems to attack the root causes of the problems.

Prevention is one of the most critical parts of healthcare, yet the most overlooked and under-budgeted.

The odds of getting killed in a plane crash are one in eleven million, but we still wear our seat belts, just in case. In the U.S., the current odds of developing diabetes as an adult are one in four, odds of developing obesity are one in three, and cancer just one in every two! The top two leading causes of death in the U.S. are heart disease and cancer!

The CDC estimates that 75% of healthcare funds are spent on chronic conditions, disabilities, and deaths that could have been prevented! We need to focus on being proactive with our bodies, as we do with wearing seat belts on planes and helmets on Harleys.

Preventive measures need to be learned and taught *before* disease; not merely to treat, but to try and *prevent* problems. Heart attack means that heart cells have died, a part of the heart (a *vital* organ) has died; for the most part, it's irreversible damage, the "hard-boiled egg syndrome." Rather than just treat heart attacks, more people should try to *prevent* heart attacks!

To beat the one-in-eleven-million odds of dying in a plane crash, you wear your seat belt. *To beat the #1 cause of death* (heart disease), or a one-in-two-chance, a fifty-fifty chance of getting cancer, an often-deadly fate, *most do absolutely nothing?!* Perhaps, they lack the knowledge to empower themselves! Thus, my mission is to empower millions with this know-how.

Physical examinations do not typically *prevent* disease, but rather *detect* disease that's already there. Exams are still advised because they can detect disease earlier.

Traditional medicine is geared at symptomatic relief only. But even though the symptoms may subside (i.e., chest pain), the underlying problem (i.e., heart blockage) is still there, silently worsening. Doctors prescribing pain medications are "masking" symptoms, not fixing them! Often modern medicine is like masking tape on a leaking garden hose, masking the problem and good for now. Meanwhile, the underlying root cause is continuing to worsen, until suddenly, the body can't handle the problem any more, breaks down and totally fails.

Medicine is based on simple algorithms that do not tend to look for the root cause nor take into account individual factors like I do.

Before I started activating my genes, I felt very achy, didn't sleep well, lacked energy, was overweight, couldn't focus and was sad.

Biohacking (i.e., "not just supplementation, but ACTIVATION"), has changed my LIFE!

Over time, I felt less achy and slept better, which, in turn, provided more energy to concentrate better. The effects seemed cumulative i.e., more and more energy, helped me lose weight, and that made me happy. I no longer needed medications and that made me even happier!

Many of my patients tell me similar success stories and that they have not felt this good in *years*! One patient said, "After many specialists, you were the first to introduce *activation, not just supplementation*, to me and I haven't felt this good in *decades!!*"

I'm extremely unique because I fuse several modalities for synergistic results and happier clientele:

- Proactive/Preventive approach to better your odds of staying healthy *before* dis-order
- Naturopathic: more natural, botanical, herbal ingredients
- Alternatives: other than expensive, traditional, synthetic, pharmaceutical drugs that often contain carcinogens, create adverse reactions, interactions, drug dependencies, toxicity and overdoses
- Functional: to attack the root cause to stop progression of dis-

order, reduce or eliminate symptoms and the need for medications

- Holistic: a whole body approach of body, mind, spirit and CELLULAR level
- Biohacking: takes control of genetic expression i.e., *not simple supplementation, but ACTIVATION of genes to re-energize, feel better and be happier*
- Integrative: integrate, or fuse in medications, if needed.

Since many doctors graduated medical school before some of the cutting edge Biohacking alternatives were available, they are not even aware of them. I now educate and collaborate (as The BioHackNP ®) with doctors, specialists and nurses.

After decades of research, I still always like to get to the cause to find the solution to rid the problem. Many of our health problems are linked to free radicals causing oxidative stress (OS). OS can lead to inflammation, per the NIH (National Institute of Health). Inflammation causes problems in the organ(s) where it accumulates i.e., breathing or memory difficulties, muscle/bone aches, autoimmune…

Dr Sanjay Gupta, Medical Correspondent for CNN, said in his book *Chasing Life* that "Oxidative stress is now linked to more than one hundred diseases!"

When we get older, there's three main internal bodily functions that age us and cause health problems.

1. *Free radicals accumulate and create damage known as oxidative stress.* OS causes inflammation i.e., an apple turning brown or rust forming on bare metal.

OS accumulates throughout our lifetime and is associated with *hundreds* of health problems, including nine of the top ten leading causes of *death* in the U.S. (strokes, cancer, diabetes, flu/pneumonia, kidney, depression/suicides, kidney, respiratory, and heart problems).

When we were younger, our bodies used to produce a lot of *antioxidants* to combat this *oxidative* stress. When we get older, our bodies are tired of producing these *vital* defenses (antioxidants), and thus produce less. As our antioxidant production decreases, it causes our OS levels to increase. This is when our health issues begin. I help my clients rev up their bodies' own production of these *antioxidants* i.e., SOD (SuperOxide Dismutase) and glutathione to drastically reduce their *oxidative* stress!

2. *Our mitochondria, the energy stations of our cells, are required for cell LIFE.* Over time, our mitochondria die off, causing cell DEATH. I teach people how to have their own body make more mitochondria for cell LIFE!

3. *Our sirtuins ("garbage men") in our body get tired of taking out so much garbage that accumulates daily, and over more years than our bodies were intended to live.* These toxins accumulate and cause toxicity. I help peoples' bodies re-activate these lazy sirtuins to detoxify.

With all natural ingredients in caplets, capsules and/or liquids, I help my clients:

1. Increase production of their own *antioxidants* to reduce *oxidative* stress.
2. Increase production of mitochondria required for cell LIFE and
3. Increase sirtuin activity to detoxify the body before toxins become toxic.

Biohacking methods may activate multiple pathways/roadways/genes (i.e., NRF1, NRF2, and NAD pathways) throughout our entire body.

Activating the NRF1 pathway increases production of mitochondria which are required for cell LIFE.

Activating the NRF2 pathway helps your body produce its own antioxidants (SOD and glutathione) that reduce OS.

Activating the NAD pathway recycles sirtuins ("garbage men") to "rid waste and toxins." Otherwise, the toxin accumulation causes toxicity and even more inflammation.

So, I thought, *'If we are helping every cell in every organ, we are helping every organ!'*

I like to call this *"not just supplementation, but ACTIVATION"* because the pathways are being *activated*, or stimulated, to accomplish *vital* cellular roles described above.

I ingest these activators, because they activate my *vital* pathways to do what they used to do and should do.

Since activating these three pathways, I look and feel like my much younger self!!

Being *proactive today* will be less costly than being *reactive tomorrow*!

Being proactive may increase not only your health span, but your lifespan!

I'm now empowering fellow healthcare professionals (HCPs) to implement my Biohacking techniques to:

- help transform themselves, their families and patients to get healthier
- create a bigger difference, a deeper impact
- educate even more HCPs
- save time
- gain financial FREEdom
- live/leave a legacy and
- be happy without the traditional job stress.

Collectively, the HCPs can transform more lives than I ever could. Thus, my mere rippling effect has accelerated into a tidal wave effect. With clients in several states, countries and continents, I'm now known as The World Wellness Expert ™

ProActive Health Tips:

- Natural foods are good; processed foods are bad.
- If it comes from the ground or has eyes, it's better.
- Shop along the inside *perimeter* of the store, where there's fruits,

vegetables, meats, and dairy. The center aisles are filled with processed foods.

- Growing your own fruit/vegetables will ensure no carcinogenic insecticides, pesticides or wax.
- Plastic is not good for you or our environment. Instead of bottled water, drink filtered water. Use BPA-free shaker bottles.
- To satisfy a sweet tooth, eat natural sweets like fruit, and pair it with protein i.e., nuts.
- Instead of artificial sweeteners, use natural honey, stevia or monk fruit.
- For earlier detection, schedule a full physical examination annually.
- To track when your annual exams are due, schedule them in your birthday month.
- Ladies (especially those over 40 or sooner if family history of breast cancer), remember your annual bilateral 3D mammography. Do NOT rely on thermography instead of mammography because it misses malignancies. If a mammography states you have dense breasts, get a bilateral ultrasound too.
- Men, schedule your annual full physical exam, including a blood test for prostate AND the annual prostate exam. If you're not comfortable with your doctor/NP performing this exam, schedule an appointment with a urologist.
- Stay active: swim, walk the dog, ride a bicycle, go for a hike, play with the kids/grandbabies outside, soccer, join a softball team, meditate, yoga…
- Find what makes you happy. As long as it's legal and morally correct, do it more! Write it in your schedule.
- If you are over age 20, your body does not make as much of the defenses it used to (i.e., antioxidants and mitochondria). Thus, *everyone over 20 (except organ recipients) should activate these vital pathways to rev up production of their bodies' good defenses.*

I empower patients, clients and healthcare professionals with Biohacking knowledge to redesign their life, be healthier and create heaven on earth!

For upcoming seminars, courses, challenges, interactive workshops, masterminds, to become a #1 International Author in my next edition of *OLO*, schedule a confidential consultation, or start Biohacking your pathways, visit *www.ShaynaMelissa.com*.

ABOUT THE AUTHOR

Shayna Melissa Stockman RN, BC-ANP, PNP, The World Wellness Expert™. Witnessing her grandmother use natural alternatives led Shayna to become a Registered Nurse (RN) for over 30 years, The BioHackNP ® and a nationally Board Certified Nurse Practitioner (NP).

After heart failure, near-death and being left hopeless by the doctors, Shayna helped heal herself and thousands of others holistically, without medications.

Shayna, licensed as an adult and child health NP, fuses a proactive naturopathic approach with BioHacking to attack the root cause. Many of her clients are off ALL medications and "haven't felt this good in YEARS" or even DECADES!

She now empowers healthcare providers with her techniques.

Her mission: help millions who were left hopeless to re-energize, feel better and be happier, often without medications.

Shayna Melissa, a Trump VIP International Award Recipient, was featured on ABC, NBC, FOX, CBS, iHeartRadio, Entertainment Tonight...Her book *Overcoming Life Obstacles* became a #1 International Bestseller, and she is now known as THE World Wellness Expert™

To feel better, create a deeper impact, or become a #1 International Best Selling Author, visit the links below:

Website: www.ShaynaMelissa.com
and www.WorldWellnessExpert.com
***LinkTree:** www.linktr.ee/Shayna_Melissa*

25

SHUNANDA SCOTT

What if I told you that you aren't alone in this crazy, miraculous, and often challenging world?

What if I told you that Angels exist and you have access to their unconditionally loving guidance in every waking moment?

What if I told you that Angels have nothing to do with religion and that EVERYONE can learn to speak with Angels?

In 2010, my life changed abruptly after the birth of my second child. Overnight, my spiritual gifts were switched on, and I found myself suddenly navigating life with my new psychic abilities.

I didn't plan on becoming an Angel Medium; I only turned to the Angels for support and protection as I began learning how to manage my newfound gifts. Truthfully, I just wanted to switch it off! I had a newborn baby, and the intensity of my psychic experiences was not only unpleasant at the time, but was often scary. I couldn't sleep without visitations from entities while I was in dream state. I couldn't go to the shops without hearing and feeling the energy of all the people around me. I was having dreams that would come true, and was suddenly seeing ghosts every-where I went!

I only began working with Archangel Michael out of desperation, in an attempt to lessen the intensity of the visions, dreams, and messages I was receiving.

I had strong resistance to working with the Angels. My feelings about mainstream religion put me off working with them for a long time. I didn't identify with the way they were portrayed in the modern spiritual and new age community; I didn't resonate with the religious images, human form, and bird-like wings. Angels didn't look like that to me! Angels appeared to me as light, colour, and frequency. As an immense and radiant auric field, resembling a rainbow, or the northern lights. And Angels certainly did not communicate with me the way religion had portrayed. For these reasons, I nearly turned away from this pathway.

The Angels had other ideas for me.

At their insistent, loving, and steadfast invitation, I began to work with them. I felt called, and it turned out that the Angelic whisper was stronger than my fear and resistance.

Over many years, I practiced, took courses, and developed my skill as an Angel Medium. At first, I worked with teachers and guides. In 2014, the Angels took over my training, and from then on, my relationship with them opened to levels I couldn't have imagined possible. What was initially a reluctant path became a journey of miracles, faith, and profound inner transformation. It became not only the journey to awakening to my mission but a guidebook for navigating my own human experience (in all its messy glory).

Working with the Angels since my awakening in 2010 has transformed my life in unimaginable ways. It is now my purpose and mission to bring the new messages from the Angels to the world and to teach people how to speak with the Angels. Now, I work with clients all around the world, helping them awaken to the infinitely loving guidance and messages from the Angels.

Today, I'd like to share with you how you can begin working with the Angels. Consider this your personal divine invitation to awaken with the Angels.

Let's begin.

Close your eyes. Slow your breathing. Feel your energy drop into your heart. Let your body soften, and your muscles relax. Now, in your mind, repeat the following invocation:

Angels, I invite you to work with me now. Please help me hear, feel, see and know your presence, in ways that I will easily understand.

Angels are not human. Angels do not have human features or a physical form.

Angels are multidimensional beings of love and light, who exist as energy and consciousness at a 9th or 10th density frequency.

Every single human has a minimum of two guardian Angels supporting them from before they incarnate, through every moment of their human life. Our Angels know us. They see our possibility, our potential, and the full picture of the path we have chosen to experience in this lifetime. They see through all our doubts and fears and accept every aspect of our expression, purpose, and experience. Without conditions.

Guardian Angels are different from Archangels, and they exist solely to support you through your own human experience. Archangels have a broader purpose, and each Archangel assists humanity through specific collective themes or focus areas.

Angels abide by certain spiritual laws. As you begin working with the Angels, you will often feel unsure about whether the message you are receiving is Angelic or your own imagination. Learning to work with the Angels is just as much a process of deconditioning and unlearning, as it is a process of remembering.

There are so many distortions ingrained into our history, our psyche, and our collective understanding of our intuition and of the Angels. And most of us have had past lives where we have been persecuted or even killed for opening up to this pathway.

And yet, here we are, moving through the biggest shift in consciousness in the entirety of human history....

It is no coincidence that the Angels are making their presence felt at this incredible time of transformation!

They want nothing more than to assist you to find your highest potential, your most profound experience of joy and bliss in this lifetime, and to remember and awaken to your innate divinity.

Every human can learn (or remember) how to speak with Angels.

It is a skill that we all can awaken to, and it can be trained with practice just like any other skill.

With one profound difference...this will completely transform your life in ways that you cannot even comprehend yet!

And inviting the Angels into your life can, and will, assist you in ways that you cannot even fathom.

When you feel the call to work with the Angels, these fears, beliefs and distortions will be presented to you. Will you choose to cross the veil, and repair your connection to the Angelic realms and the divine?

You are 100% safe to work with the Angels. You are 100% to awaken to your powerful intuitive abilities. It is your innate birthright to use your powerful intuition. It is your innate birthright to receive the powerful and loving guidance of your Angelic team. And with time and practice, it can become as easy as any other form of communication!

Learning to speak with Angels is not as hard as you think. With practice and understanding some simple rules about the tone and energy around Angelic messages, you will become more and more confident hearing and receiving their messages.

How do you know you are receiving an Angelic message, and that it's not your imagination?

You will use your intuition to receive Angelic messages. This means you will use your clairvoyance, clairsentience, claircognizance, and clairaudience to receive, and decode Angelic messages. Think of yourself as a translator, learning a new language for the first time. Except this language is one that only YOU can decipher and requires you to trust and have faith in both the mode of delivery and the message received.

It can feel strange at first. Was that an Angelic message? Or am I imagining things?

It is very common to expect to "hear" or "see" Angels as an external voice or presence. It's actually much more subtle than that, to begin with...

It's a whisper. A feeling. A sense of love flowing through your heart, and a thought that appears in your mind as if you are remembering a conversation from the past.

The difference between an Angelic message, and your own imagination is very subtle and nuanced at first. The only way to know for sure if you are receiving Angelic messages is to TRUST them. The more you trust what you receive, the stronger your ability to discern them becomes.

Angelic messages have a very distinct tone, that is actually very different from your own inner voice. Once you know the rules of how Angels must engage and interact with us, it makes it much easier to trust the messages that you receive:

- Angels love you without limits.
- Angels will never scare you, shame you, judge you, talk down to you, or laugh at you.
- Angels accept you unconditionally.
- Angels will NEVER ask you to do something against your free will.
- Angels do not predict the future, and will never reveal the purpose or outcome of a situation (this would violate the miracle of your human experience).
- Angels help you see the path that is hidden.
- Angels always feel loving, validating, comforting, and safe.

The Angels are here with us now as we move through the most significant shift in consciousness in the entirety of human experience on earth.

The Angels bring messages of hope, connection, and love, as we navigate a shift from separation to unity.

The Angels are here to help YOU awaken to your own divine mission: to embody the new frequency of 5D as it is emerging in your own consciousness. To birth 5D in your own reality.

The following words are a channelled message from the Angels on the themes of unity consciousness, and the current ascension journey.

Channelled Angel Message on Unity Consciousness:

We bring you messages on unity.

As you expand your awareness now, we ask you to bring into your energy field, and heart, these messages on unity. Know that this transmission is both mind- and heart-activating and that you can safely allow the frequencies encoded in this transmission to enter your heart field.

As the collective consciousness shifts to 5D, there are new energies in the form of light flooding earth in waves.

As a lightworker, you will experience the new energy first. Once you have integrated the new light, your frequency will then expand and support the collective frequency shift. For all are connected, and as you heal, love, and expand into new awareness, so you help the many heal, love, and expand into new awareness.

As you explore the transmission themes, they will activate in your own life and relationships, for you to process.

Your own expansion and integration of each wave of ascension, and its lessons, will have a profound effect on the collective frequency shift.

The current frequency shift includes many themes, one being unity.

As the collective explores unity, it also sees everywhere that there is DIS-unity. And so, you will notice both in your own life and in your understanding of global experience, that there is a light being shone now on all that is DIS-unity.

We ask you to pay attention to all that you identify in yourself and in your collective experience that is division, separation, judgment, and self-righteousness. We ask you to notice all that creates disagreement, conflict, and disharmony. This is the trigger. The awareness of dis-unity shows you your own shadow and the collective shadow.

These are not bad. They ARE.

The human experience is one of polarity.

In order to explore unity and co-create from this place, one must understand its shadow.

Do you see that all that is occurring now in the world is allowing the collective consciousness to explore unity via exploration of dis-unity?

This is the beginning of the frequency shift to unity consciousness!

This is not the first time this theme has been explored. It has been explored many times in the entirety of the human experience.

And it is being explored now with an accelerated focus as a very large number of conscious human thought forms are now actively exploring this theme from a place of observation, rather than identification.

As you identify with the experience of dis-unity, you will experience pain, grief, anger, sadness, and hopelessness, as you will experience dis-unity as that which is happening to you.

As you observe the experience of dis-unity within yourself and the collective, you will notice your emotional triggers and allow yourself to practice compassion, forgiveness, healing and acceptance.

In one experience that holds a three-dimensional frequency, you will react from your wound.

In another experience that holds a five-dimensional frequency, you will react from your heart.

There is no right or wrong experience, and you will move between both, and this is necessary in order to fully explore unity/dis-unity.

In order to anchor unity consciousness through your own heart field and so the collective field, all aspects must be understood and integrated, within self and collective.

You seek unity consciousness.

The fastest pathway to that which you seek is to explore lack of unity consciousness, within your own awareness and experience.

As you find peace and acceptance within your own heart for how you have expressed dis-unity, so you assist the collective to also find peaceful acceptance and understanding of dis-unity.

You have no control over that which is outside of yourself, other than shifting your own awareness and perception. And so, your most powerful way to serve the many is serve yourself first, and then serve the many from this place of healing.

Unity consciousness is acceptance of other even when the actions of other are in disagreement with your beliefs.

Unity consciousness is love of other even when another has beliefs, actions, or words that are opposite to yours.

Unity consciousness is connected via empathy, love, and non-judgement.

Unity consciousness is complete acceptance.

Unity consciousness is respect for the sovereignty of all living beings.

Unity consciousness is radiant love of self and other. Unity consciousness is expanded frequency.

Unity consciousness is not righteous. Unity consciousness understands that there is no right or wrong, only experience .The exploration of unity consciousness is the exploration of love.

As you explore unity and dis-unity, your heart will open to unity connection. We invite you to explore unity consciousness.

Channelled Angel Message on the current Ascension journey:

We speak to you about the pathway of ascension. Ascension is but one word to describe the journey of conscious enlightenment. Ascension is an inner heart journey to light/love.

There is a universal experience now, of awakening. This awakening is both individual and collective.

The awakening to consciousness journey has always existed. Many have walked this path before. Many walk this path collectively now.

The ascension journey is inwards; it is both a heart and a mind journey.

As you walk this journey, you will experience realisation. There is no end point. This journey is a practice. Realisation is a constant shifting state of awareness.

Realisation will trigger expansion of consciousness. Expansion of consciousness will trigger realisation. This is a cyclical, gradual frequency expansion, a spiral with both a linear and outwards/upwards motion.

Ascension is journeyed by the one, and the many.

As the one journeys within to find self realisation, so, the one experiences a shift in consciousness, and in unison the collective experiences change and transformation. As everything is connected.

As you journey inwards to heal yourself, find the light, and awaken your radiant joy, so, the collective also heals, finds the light, and awakens to radiant joy.

The collective expansion of consciousness is under way, via individual self realisation.

For those of you who seek to serve the collective, and are called to service now, we say that the fastest way to serve the many is to journey inwards, and experience your own transformation and ascension.

All that you do within ripples outwards, as that which you describe as the butterfly effect.

The spiral pathway of ascension explores both darkness and light in search of fluid balance. It is a dynamic, ever moving wave and dance, as full expression of self is never constant. The human journey is full spectrum, with all emotions and experiences required in order to self actualise and ascend.

The journey of ascension is a discovery of all that is an aspect of you and realising full self expression.

It is an awakening, reclaiming and integration of self.

It is finding places where you experience dis-unity, and moving towards unity.

It is finding ways where you are unloving, and practicing compassion, acceptance and forgiveness.

It is finding ways in which you feel anger, pain, sadness, grief, and becoming curious as to the cause.

On this journey you realise that no other is responsible for your pain, and no other holds the key to your happiness. Both are found within. You hold the key to your experience.

Ascension is a journey that requires a sacred guide, indeed many sacred guides. Your sacred guides appear in many forms, at the exact right time, to assist, witness, activate, and light the pathway for you.

Your sacred guide has walked the journey to darkness already, and sees you in your full sovereignty to witness and support you as you walk your own path. Your sacred guide empowers, and awakens the healer within you, by sharing their own healing journey.

Your sacred guide does not claim sovereignty over your healing, your knowledge, or your intuition.

We invite you to become curious and discerning about your ascension journey, and work only with those who activate your sovereignty. Likewise we invite you to practice sovereignty to other, as you begin to activate those for whom you are the sacred guide.

The ascension blueprint is one of love. The pathway is inwards via your heart. In order to become a conscious wanderer on your own sacred journey, we invite you to become aware of all that is love, and all that is not love within your own frequency.

We invite you to seek healing as you need it and to choose the pathway of compassion, acceptance and forgiveness of self, and of other.

We invite you to become conscious of the actions that best support you to activate love in your heart, and in your life, and equally, we invite you to become curious of all that lowers your frequency, and feels fearful and despairing. Conscious awareness is a daily practice that will support you through your ascension journey.

That which raises your frequency:

Music and sound, meditation, chakra meditation, being in nature, moving your body in ways that you enjoy, drinking pure filtered water, eating organic fruits and vegetables, pure organic essences, oils and sprays, roses and other flowers that bring you joy, laughing, hugging & physical touch, eye gazing, making love, connecting with friends family and loved ones, sleep, the ocean, singing, helping another, helping many, expressing yourself, healing your wounds and shadow, creativity, using your imagination, being with animals, learning about topics that interest you, compassion, acceptance, forgiveness, joy, love, being you.

That which lowers your frequency:

Television, radio, movies, internet, social media, chemicals in food, chemicals in water, fluoride, drugs that are used as disconnection mechanisms, sugar, meat & animal products, isolation, disconnection, lack of movement, lack of self expression, disassociation, abandonment of self, denial, judgment, superiority, control, attachment, violence whether expressed or viewed, trauma whether experienced or viewed, electronic radiation and magnetic fields, anger, rage, resentment, blame, guilt, shame, and lack of love.

We invite you to become conscious of the linear, upwards and outwards spiral motion of your own ascension journey and practice compassion, acceptance and forgiveness of self and other as you integrate your full expression of self to become self-realised.

With love,
The Angels,
& Shunanda

ABOUT THE AUTHOR

Angel medium, ascension guide and mother of three Shunanda Scott is passionate about teaching people how to receive the infinitely loving guidance and support of the Angels.

Upon the birth of her second child, Shunanda experienced a spiritual awakening and began learning how to manage her newly discovered intuitive abilities. For years Shunanda trained with mentors, teachers, and the Angels themselves, and now works with starseeds and light workers all over the world from her beach home in Sydney.

The New Angel Messages is a collection of sacred daily Angel transmissions received by Shunanda, each message sent with love to guide humanity through the current collective journey of transformation and awakening.

Website: www.shunanda.co
Email: angels@shunanda.co
Facebook: www.facebook.com/shunanda
Instagram: www.instagram.com/_shunanda_

SILKE HARVEY

AWAKENING

"She runs through the forest
Luscious scents stroking her skin
Naked body celebrating the sky
Ice cold winds caressing her body
Freedom in every rustling leaf
She runs through the forest
Exalted exhilaration thrilling her senses
Ecstasy in every breath
She pulls the moon from the sky
Together they dance the dance of the Sisterhood
To the ancient song of the trees and the Earth
Accompanied by the pounding drums of stags
And the soothing sounds of fairies
They dance upon a mound of rotten bones
Supported by ancestors of aeons past
She runs through the forest
Pure exhilaration

And love and awe for her own womanhood
She runs free
No longer weighed down by society's chains
Placed on her without her consent
Here in the forest she is wild and free
Just like the owls and the eagles
Like every leaf on every tree
She runs through the forest
Light as a feather
She kneels and drinks deeply
Drinks her fill from an enchanted stream
The forest is alive
Magick is alive
The winds are howling
The sky is dark
The stars and moon are shining fiercely
It is a wild night
And she is Yaga
She is a powerful Goddess
She owns the forest
She owns the wind
She owns the stars
She owns the moon
She owns the Universe
Deep and mysterious
And the forest owns her
And the wind owns her
And the stars own her
And the moon owns her
And the Universe owns her
And all becomes one
All is one
She is one with the Earth
The Earth is one with her
Her consciousness expands

And the Universe welcomes her back into Her gentle embrace
Long lost Daughter
And as her consciousness expands so does her sense of freedom
She is at one with all there is
All off creation
In this deep dark wild forest
She is her true self
She is her very essence
She is Yaga
And she is enough"

T he day I fell asleep on the keyboard of my laptop is the day that awakened the Yaga in me.

Baba Yaga: feared and barbaric Slavic Goddess and reviled, wicked witch. Yet none of society's prejudices are based on truth. The Yaga is the wild side of the Goddess—the deep, dark forest, howling winds, death and rebirth, just like the Celtic Cerridwen. And she is the wise and wild old crone, the one who will not be tamed by society's preconceptions of how women should be.

The day I fell asleep after working a gruelling 16-hour stretch for the seventh week in a row without a single day off is branded into my mind. It is the day that changed everything.

"Where am I?" The question burned itself into my befuddled, dazed consciousness. It took quite some time for me to realise that I'd fallen asleep at my desk. When the realisation came, it hit me like a hammer blow. I cried so hard that it felt like I would carry on crying for the rest of my life.

Years of working first as a financial translator for one of the Big Four, then as a freelancer still servicing the "Big Boys" had broken my free spirit. Cruel deadlines and expectations beyond what any healthy human mind could conceive had eroded my very essence. I mourned my younger, carefree, happy self who used to play bass in a Rock'n'Roll band for a living and had the fun of a lifetime doing so. Now, all that was left was work.

Circumstances had forced me to enter the corporate world just to pay the bills. I had no love for the work I was doing. Life seemed barely worth it on that fateful day.

But during my darkest hour, a small voice at the back of my head started whispering. It gently reminded me of my skills. I had been attuned to Reiki many years ago but had all but forgotten about it. Thinking that it couldn't hurt to try, I dusted off my old skill and started treating myself.

It worked. I began to focus on energy healing, getting certified as a Reiki Master, Chakra Dancing practitioner, Reiki Drum practitioner and animal healer. I went to a Tibetan monastery in Scotland, the largest in the world outside of Tibet, and learnt how to practice mindfulness from the monks.

With a new spring in my step, I started a Reiki practice and loved every minute of it. Then, when the pandemic struck, I took my business online, founding the Inner Hippie Club, a place where I taught women how to reclaim their Inner Hippie, that carefree teenage feeling before life got serious. I shared everything I had learnt.

Meanwhile, I was deepening my connection to the Yaga. I started to feel a close kinship. This woman is wild and free. She lives life on her own terms and speaks her truth. She doesn't care for beauty standards or what everyone thinks of her. She is authentic to the bone.

As I am entering the crone stage of my life, I aspire to be like the Yaga —authentic and free-spirited. And I want other women to find the courage to reclaim their authentic selves, too. That is why I founded Inner Hippie Books, a publishing house and virtual fireside where powerful stories are shared. Because the pen is mightier than the sword. Because stories change the world.

The time for silence is over. The world is changing and moving into a new, lighter vibration. But the change is not easy. It is a difficult, nasty transition that is bringing a lot of hurt and pain to the surface. The poison needs to be spilt so that Gaya and all of her children can start to heal.

Every day I talk to Yaga. She is on my celestial team and cheering me on, reminding me of the importance of being Yaga—wild, free, and unapologetically YOU.

ABOUT THE AUTHOR

Silke Harvey is the founder of the Inner Hippie Club and Inner Hippie Books, radio presenter, international bestselling author, Senior Level Executive Contributor at Brainz Magazine, Brainz 500 Global 2020 and 2021 honoree and CREA Global Awards 2022 nominee. Her life's mission is to help strong and amazing women speak their truth and be heard and leave this world a better place for generations of children to come.

Drawing on her colourful past as an energy healer, Rock'n'Roll bass player, corporate employee, and freelance financial translator, she has compiled her wealth of personal and professional knowledge into the Inner Hippie Club to help other women find joy and purpose again.

Inner Hippie Books is a natural extension of the Inner Hippie Club, providing all thought leaders, visionaries and change-makers with a virtual fireside to share their stories.

Silke is also a certified Reiki Master, Reiki Drum and Seichem Level II practitioner, a graduate of the Diploma in Chakra Dancing and Creative Meditation, HAO Diploma in Animal Healing and HAOK9 Massage, and a member of the Healing Animals Organisation.

She lives in the UK with her wonderful husband and her rescue dog and splits her time between her cosy home by the coast in North East England and her beautiful country cottage in Bulgaria where she is planning to run retreats. To join the exclusive Sisters of Yaga circle, contact Silke directly at her email below.

Email: *silke@innerhippiebooks.com*
Website: *www.innerhippiebooks.com*

TIFFANIE YAEL MAOZ, PH.D.

ACCEPTING TRANSFORMATION: YOU ARE A MULTI-DIMENSIONAL, EVER-EVOLVING INDIVIDUAL CAPABLE OF MAKING AN IMPACT THROUGH A VARIETY OF MEDIUMS

YOUR DEGREE DOES NOT DEFINE YOU

Having a Ph.D. can be both a badge of honor and its own heavy burden.** I know you may be thinking "Yeah, yeah. Cry me a river." And yet just like any other title, people recognize it and assume it indicates that your life is somehow preordained, predestined, and so your path in life is easy, or at least fairly straightforward. Now, this may well be the case for a select few, but there is often a heavy dose of shock and antidepressants for new graduates as they grapple with the reality of finding their way and defining themselves.

Most people choose to get a Ph.D. because they have an altruistic nature within them. Perhaps you're also like this. There's something within you that longs to make the world a better place, to explore its wonders and share it with the rest of the world. You're driven to create new innovations to improve the world and make it a better place to live in.

But this altruism can also shackle and tie you down. Society often dictates what you can and cannot become for good or ill based on the way you define yourself.

When I received my Ph.D. in plant genomics, many of us believed that the most honorable work was in academia, teaching, or the non-profit sector—aiding underprivileged people around the world. To deviate from this path would label you as greedy and self-centered.

But as everyone knows, academic positions are quite scarce and highly sought after, leaving them to the research rock stars, with the rest of us mortals left to find work as lab managers or *gasp* in startups.

I won't sugarcoat it: my self-esteem and even my desire to make a difference in the world initially took a hit. My story is that I took the startup path for more than 5 years, and I'm so grateful for it.

Being in an environment where I could experiment with lots of other skills—project management, product development, communication, sales, operations, and marketing was a wonderland of opportunity. I found my value on a team and the business world extended my knowledge beyond academic research.

By sharing my gifts and talents and being fully myself—with post-it note planning sessions, whiteboard brainstorming, creative presentations to clients, and coffees with prospects—I learned that I really love business and at my core, I enjoy working with good people that want to do good things in this world.

When you try new things, meet new people, get to know yourself, and enjoy being with yourself, you'll see that society can't limit who you are and what you can become. You are a blended amalgam of amazing gifts, talents, and experiences that makes this world a better place.

ACCEPTING YOUR EVOLUTION

The COVID lockdown made me realize that this was my opportunity to build the family-work life I had only dreamed of, one where I could be available to my kids whenever they needed me, without having to share personal details and ask permission from anyone. This freed me from the self-limitation of being the researcher and expert, and allowed me to return to being the student, teacher, partner, or creative person in the room.

I realized that I wanted to mentor other women from STEM backgrounds like me. They had great ideas but didn't know how to move forward or evaluate their merit. Then it dawned on me how to go about doing this: assembling female innovators, teachers, and therapists to share how they see the changing world of women's health. I wanted to give women around the world a voice and platform for education and empowerment. I also realized that I had a soft spot for people in my parent's generation—entrepreneurs now approaching or having recently entered retirement yet not ready to laze away their days sitting back in their rocking chairs. These active creators were eager to continue growing their businesses. Realizing that the technology, tools, and strategies that I learned working with a startup could also be applied to small business scenarios was really eye-opening and showed me yet again that I am more than my degree... I'm my experience, my compassion, my inspiration, my family, my culture, and my worldview.

And it's the same for you. Take the first step and identify who it is you want to be. Reach out to lovingly accept the part of you that desires something 'more'. This doesn't mean that you aren't grateful for the people in your life now or the work you have that pays your bills; it means that you are ready to grow and make those changes for you to evolve.

Now, I'm a fairly practical sort, and I like to have at least a semblance of a plan. So whether you're transforming from a baker to a motivational speaker, a building contractor to a draftsman, or a scientist to a book publisher, remember that you are not just a title. You are a unique person ready to give back. You are a creator. And by honoring your desire to transform, you inspire others to give back more in creative ways as well.

MAKING YOUR IMPACT

My transformation happened when I realized that as much as I loved business coaching and consulting, I wanted to be more 'hands-on' in helping my clients. I really enjoy strategizing new ways to streamline their processes and get more customers into their pipelines. But at the same time, I felt slightly bereft when leaving it to them to take action.

Initially, I did a small pivot to working as a fractional COO, someone you could hire to do all the strategizing with you and get in to actually do the work to get the projects moving along. It was on one of these projects that I realized the best move my client could make for their business was to create a book. This would enable them to further build their brand, solidify their authority, and bring in more customers to their business. We also just thought it would be fun.

What can I say? I fell in love with book publishing and decided that here was the perfect medium for me to continue to work with and support startups and small businesses while creating a tangible product with them, as a partner in the process, that would spread the word of their business and enable them to do more good in this world.

Today, I'm a scientist who writes and publishes books—and I'm having a ball. It's my fervent hope that more scientists, mathematicians, engineers, and other technologists will explore new ways of expressing their creativity and intellect, merging their expertise with their art. Some scientists are now communications consultants, others have become artists, and yet others have founded new startups and become business leaders in their own right.

When you allow yourself to transform to what really feels right at a soul level, you know in your heart that you're on the right path. There is a serenity and satisfaction that comes with it, where it just feels right. You may not be an expert at the beginning or have all the connections, but know in your gut that it will come. That the right things will always come for you at the right time. You can learn, grow, and evolve while making your impact.

ABOUT THE AUTHOR

Dr. Maoz has led both international scientific and business projects generating millions of dollars in revenue. For the past 7 years, she's worked with small business owners and startup founders to position their products and develop their services for the people that need them most. Today she and her team at Beverly House Press help entrepreneurs connect with the right audience for their business through the medium of books.

With a fast and easy author on-boarding and support program and exclusive 1:1 business strategy planning, Dr. Maoz and her team are helping entrepreneurs tell their stories, share their wisdom, and realize their dreams of running a successful business. They specialize in serving the needs of entrepreneurs that want to create books that strategically position them and their business to get more clients with ease, and that want support and advice for implementing the backend tech to bring these new clients into their world in just a few months.

Download the FREE guide to Marketing That Pays For Itself at her website below:

Website: *www.beverlyhousepress.com/sacred*
Facebook: *www.facebook.com/tiffanieyaelmaoz*
and www.facebook.com/BeverlyHousePress

ABOUT AMA PUBLISHING

& ADRIANA MONIQUE ALVAREZ

"Writing a book is sacred. It's not easy, nor is it difficult. It is a holy act."
~Adriana Monique Alvarez

B eing a life path number 3 means I have deep reverence for a clear vision, imagination, and the joy of living. Creativity and self-expression are my right and left hand.

So, it makes sense that my soul thrives when I am assisting others in communicating the stories that matter to them.

As entrepreneurs, there's an added layer—our stories literally call in the people who we are meant to work with.

I am the first woman in my family to put my knowledge, experience, and wisdom in books that can be passed down through generations.

I suspect you might be a first as well.

This is a sacred calling.

It's been said that 85% of the population have the desire to write a book, but only 1% actually write and publish it.

The Mayans were a Mesoamerican civilization, noted for Maya script, the only known fully developed writing system of the pre-Columbian Americas, as well as for its art, architecture, mathematical and astronomical systems.

Their writing system was made up of 800 glyphs. Some of the glyphs were pictures and others represented sounds. They chiseled the glyphs into stone and inside codices.

Codices were books that were folded like an accordion. The pages were fig bark covered in white lime and bound in jaguar skins. The Mayans wrote hundreds of these books. They contained information on history, medicine, astronomy, and their religion. The Spanish missionaries burned all but four of these books.

The Ancient Mayans were a very religious people. Mayan actions were based on rituals and ceremonies.

I have been asked to return to the rituals and ceremonies that activate and invoke the writer within those who are being asked to write and release their stories in the world right now.

The first step is leaving the distractions that keep us busy, occupied, and convinced we don't have the resources—be it time, money, or energy —to write a book.

The second step is to connect to ourselves, the book that is calling us, and those who will read it.

The third step is action that is surrounded by support.

You don't need to know how to write and publish your book.

You don't need to know how to market your book.

You don't need to know how to make money from your book.

You simply must know YOU MUST DO IT.

You must know this is not a "someday" thing.

It's a "right now, sense of urgency, surrendering to the call" thing.

· · ·

In December of 2016 I published my first book, *"Success Re-defined: Travel, Motherhood and Being the Boss."*

That book is what launched my online business. I had been offline before that and it allowed me to get 35 wonderful clients, right off the bat. It then led to me getting featured in publications like Forbes, International Living, and The Huffington Post, and I then went on to run a program just six months later that had over 100 clients in it.

Right after that I really felt this strong urge to help women write their own book and figure out how to get featured in publications just like I had done, so I ran a program called "Instant Authority" and it was magical... it was all clicking and coming together and I had plans of running and transitioning my business to where the focus would be on books and helping women communicate in a really powerful way.

However, just a few months later I found out there were major complications with my third pregnancy, and I would later go on to lose that baby.

From that point on, all I have done is put one foot in front of the other. I've done my best to show up every single day to live this life in her honor, remembering to really be present with the two children that I do have with me, to having a wonderful relationship with my husband, and to pouring my heart into my clients and my business.

It was in April, 2019 that I felt like it was time to take the stream that had went dormant and bring it back, and it was an interesting thing because I had hired a new coach at that time, and she said, "I think you should move in the direction of books, and that you should make this part of your business model."

I ran with her idea because it was the confirmation that I needed, and since that time I have sold over 50 spots in these book collaborations.

This has been an amazing journey and what I want you to know is that this is what happens when you keep following your heart and keep putting one foot in front of the other.

There are times when entrepreneurship and business and dreams in life can be all over the place, but the key is that we stay on the path.

Sometimes I think, "Why was this two-year detour part of my journey? What was that all about?"

And what I hear is that the people who were meant to be in the books with me, they weren't in my life yet, and I was not yet the woman who was going to lead them through those difficult times.

I was forced to dig deep, I was forced to find my most authentic voice, and now it's that much sweeter.

Since I've been announcing the books, I've had a lot of men approach me who want to be in books as well.

When I was doing business consulting, I was really honoring the unique differences between men and women and how I could help women through both motherhood and business and navigating that and now I'm so excited to be opening the books up to have male contributors as well.

Adriana Monique Alvarez (AMA) Publishing would love to help you tell your story too. We have helped to publish authors through our course, through our multi-author books, and as solo authors.

Here's the thing… **Your story, it's ready to be told**.

Website: www.AdrianaMoniqueAlvarez.com
Facebook: www.facebook.com/AdrianaMoniqueAlvarez
Youtube: www.youtube.com/c/AdrianaMoniqueAlvarez